WHISPERS
FROM
A STORM

WHISPERS FROM A STORM

Fragments from a Japanese Esperantist in China during the Second Sino-Japanese War

HASEGAWA TERU (VERDA MAJO)

TRANSLATED BY ADAM KUPLOWSKY

UNIVERSITY OF HAWAI'I PRESS
Honolulu

© 2025 University of Hawai'i Press
All rights reserved
Printed in the United States of America

First printed, 2025

Library of Congress Cataloging-in-Publication Data

Names: Hasegawa, Teru (Verda Majo), 1912-1947, author. | Kuplowsky, Adam, translator.
Title: Whispers from a storm : fragments from a Japanese Esperantist in China during the Second Sino-Japanese War / Teru Hasegawa ; translated by Adam Kuplowsky.
Other titles: Fragments from a Japanese Esperantist in China during the Second Sino-Japanese War
Description: Honolulu : University of Hawai'i Press, [2025] | Includes bibliographical references and index.
Identifiers: LCCN 2024045638 (print) | LCCN 2024045639 (ebook) | ISBN 9780824899639 (hardback) | ISBN 9780824899660 (epub) | ISBN 9780824899677 (kindle edition) | ISBN 9780824899653 (pdf)
Subjects: LCSH: Hasegawa, Teru, 1912-1947—Translations into English. | Sino-Japanese War, 1937-1945—China—Personal narratives, Japanese. | Fascism—History—20th century. | Esperantists—Biography. | Esperanto—History.
Classification: LCC DS777.5315 .H36 2025 (print) | LCC DS777.5315 (ebook) | DDC 940.53092 [B]—dc23/eng/20241213
LC record available at https://lccn.loc.gov/2024045638
LC ebook record available at https://lccn.loc.gov/2024045639

Cover and frontispiece: Hasegawa Teru, circa 1929, when she was enrolled at the Nara Higher Normal School for Girls. Source: Nara Hasegawa Teru no Kai.

University of Hawai'i Press books are printed on acid-free paper and meet the guidelines for permanence and durability of the Council on Library Resources.

[This book] is an artefact from the ordinary life
of an ordinary woman, yet it also reflects a
miniature of our times. In it, the author, a young
Esperantist, has issued a righteous call, one that
has boiled up from her heart, after having
witnessed, with her own eyes, the butchery,
burning, and senseless bombing of China by the
militarists of her homeland. The call is not a loud
one, and yet it rises like a banner of human
justice, like an emblem of "love and hate."

—Liu Ren, foreword to *Flustr' el uragano*
(A Whisper from a Storm), by Hasegawa Teru

Contents

Acknowledgments	ix
A Note on Names and Terms	xi
Translator's Introduction:	
An Extraordinary "Ordinary Woman"	1
The Dove of Peace by Elpin	24

PART I: INSIDE FIGHTING CHINA — 27

1. Inside Fighting China	29
2. Two Lost Apples	101
3. May in the Capital City	106

PART II: TO ESPERANTO LAND — 111

4. Love and Hate	113
5. Victory for China Is the Key to Tomorrow for All of Asia	116
6. To All the Esperantists of the World	120
7. If Winter Comes, Can Spring Be Far Behind?	127
8. Esperanto and Democracy	131
9. The Misfortune of a Democratic World	133

PART III: ON FASCIST JAPAN — 137

10. Japan—A Nation under Barbarous Rule	139
11. An Age of Substitutes—Vignettes of Wartime Japan	144
12. Women Workers in Wartime Japan	149
13. A Profile of Japanese Students	161
14. Japan at a Crossroads	168
Further Readings	175
Index	179

Acknowledgments

I owe many thanks to many people who supported me during the translation and assembly of this collection, first of all to Stephanie Chun for taking a chance on it. Your patience and sound editorial advice have allowed me to furnish a manuscript that I can feel truly proud of. Likewise, I owe thanks to Wendy Lawrence for all the hard work she put into copyediting the book. I am equally indebted to Tanabe Minoru, Nakanishi Toshiko, and Terajima Toshio, all of whom, in addition to supplying me with various primary- and secondary-source documents, sent me many pleasant emails and sincere words of encouragement. Furthermore, I extend my appreciation to the Nara Hasegawa Teru no Kai as a whole, for their support of this project. Multan dankon, samideanoj!

A book is nothing without its readers, and I would like to acknowledge mine, especially Luke Kuplowsky, Dylan McNeil, Humphrey Tonkin, and the University of Hawai'i Press anonymous peer reviewers, who generously gave their time to look over and comment on my manuscript at various stages. Likewise, it would be terribly remiss of me not to mention Juwen Zhang, Fan Wu, and Chang Yuchen for answering questions about the Chinese poetry and songs that appear throughout.

Finally, I would like to thank my wife, Jessica, whose caring soul, curious mind, and love of reading are among the reasons I strive to find interesting stories to translate—stories that I hope will contribute to building a kinder, more equitable world.

A Note on Names and Terms

Throughout the translation of this collection, I have made an effort to standardize various names and terms for the sake of clarity. Where identification was possible, abbreviated names and pseudonyms have been replaced with actual names—for example, Liu (Ren) rather than L., Ye Laishi rather than Ĵelezo. Chinese names and places have generally been rendered in Pinyin according to their Mandarin pronunciation, with the exception of Hong Kong, yum cha, and the names of some well-known historical figures and organizations such as Chiang Kai-shek and the Kuomintang. Furthermore, the names of geographic locations have been updated to their modern, established spellings, such as Taiwan instead of Formosa and Guangzhou instead of Canton, unless historically relevant. Last, the names of Chinese, Japanese, and Esperanto magazines and organizations have been transliterated rather than translated, unless integral to narrative comprehension.

TRANSLATOR'S INTRODUCTION
An Extraordinary "Ordinary Woman"

What does it mean to love one's country? Is patriotism demonstrated by unthinking allegiance to the state? Or is it an active engagement, like love itself, requiring constant effort and occasional conflict? What does it mean to fight for freedom? Does it mean to fight for one's own prosperity at the expense of others' welfare? Or is it the pursuit of a communal, borderless freedom, guided by a spirit of universal justice? And what does it mean to stand in solidarity with another? Is it merely a gesture of sympathy? Or is it an active undertaking of learning and unlearning, not only inclusive but transcendent, leading toward an ever-widening network of cooperation and shared struggle?

These questions repeatedly present themselves to readers of Hasegawa Teru—also known as Verda Majo—a Japanese Esperantist and human rights activist who left her native land in the 1930s to join the Chinese resistance against the Japanese Imperial Army. As an Esperantist with pacifist, transnationalist ideals, she risked both comfort and security in her effort to call out injustice, oppression, and hypocrisy where she saw it, urging her compatriots to come to their senses at a time when the world, in the name of "patriotism" and "prosperity," was hurtling toward bloody bedlam.

Hasegawa Teru was born on March 7, 1912, to a middle-class family in Yamanashi Prefecture. The second of three children, her future reputation as an outspoken critic and nonconformist may have been divined from a young age. As her older sister, Yukiko, recalled: "From birth, Teru was stubborn and staunchly rebellious. Once she started crying, she would howl so loud one feared her throat would split, and she wouldn't stop, no matter how one tried to console her. However, after she had sufficiently cried her heart out, she would suddenly regain her calm, like the sky after a typhoon."[1] Showing little interest in dolls, young Teruko preferred to roughhouse with sticks and stones, with a healthy dose of humor and a keen wit that made her popular with others.

Between 1913 and 1922, her father, a civil engineer, moved their family to Tokyo, Saitama, and back to Tokyo, where she spent her school years. In 1929 she graduated from the Tokyo Prefectural Third Higher School for Girls and enrolled in the Japanese Literature Department at the Nara Higher Normal School for Girls, with the intention of becoming a teacher. Her main reason for choosing Nara, the country's ancient capital, was likely because it gave her an opportunity to escape her conservative family, especially her father and brother, with whom she had increasingly come into conflict during her high school years. According to Yukiko, diary entries from this period suggest that she became distrustful of society in general and antagonistic toward men and symbols of authority, her feelings growing so strong that she once planned to commit suicide—feelings she later fashioned into a short story titled "Spring Madness" (Printempa frenezo).[2]

While living semi-independently in a student dormitory in Nara, Hasegawa enjoyed visiting shrines and temples, traveled extensively, and developed such a compulsion for reading that she was rarely seen without a book in her hands.[3] In spite of her cavalier attitude toward studying and her frequent absences from school, her classmates saw that she possessed "a brilliant mind, capable of grasping the heart of lectures in a way that inspired delight and fear in her teachers."[4] She was a member of her school's tanka club and wrote poems and semi-autobiographical stories that were well received by her peers. From behind her bookish jam-jar glasses flickered a pair of passionate eyes that closely observed the world around and beyond her immediate environs.

During summer vacation in 1931, Yukiko introduced Hasegawa to the international auxiliary language of Esperanto. Invented by Polish ophthalmologist L. L. Zamenhof in 1873, Esperanto was intended to relieve the "heavy burden of linguistic differences" that its creator saw as engendering social conflict on local, national, and international levels.[5] With its simple grammar and "international" vocabulary, it was promoted as a tool for nonhierarchical communication and motivated by an "internal idea" of "brotherhood and justice among all peoples."[6] Although its inventor advanced it as a politically neutral language, leftist activists in Europe and East Asia after World War I used it as a radical medium for connecting the various and geographically separated struggles of the global proletariat.

Popular in Japan since 1906, by the 1920s and early 1930s Esperanto had won the widespread support of progressive circles in the country looking to strengthen ties with international worker, socialist, communist, and anarchist movements. Several leftist organizations, like the Zen Nihon Musansha Geijutsu Renmei, and journals, like *Bungaku annai,* even adopted Esperanto names (Nippona Proleta Artista Federacio and *La literatura gvido,* respectively) to express their committed internationalism. When Hasegawa began studying Esperanto in earnest at the Nara Esperanto Association in May 1932, the international auxiliary language introduced her to a large and politically charged transnational community, and with that must have come a feeling of responsibility to pay attention to global events—notably, the rise of fascism in Europe and East Asia. Increasingly, she became less interested in poetry and more interested in politics.

Coinciding with Hasegawa's growing interest in Esperanto and its internationalist outlook were several key events signaling Japan's descent into fascism. These included the March

4 Translator's Introduction

15 and April 16 incidents of 1928–1929, which involved widespread crackdowns on socialist, communist, and other leftist groups; the Manchurian Incident of 1931, a false-flag operation staged by the Japanese army as a pretext to invade the Chinese mainland; and Prime Minister Inukai Tsuyoshi's assassination in 1932 by Japanese naval officers, part of a failed coup d'état that nevertheless marked the end of civilian control over Japan's political affairs. Amid these more conspicuous events, various court rulings subverted the normative structures of the state, as in Nazi Germany and Fascist Italy.[7] While historians of Japan have long debated the semantics regarding whether Japan's dominant political ideology in the prewar and war years was, in fact, "fascist," internationalists like Hasegawa quickly connected the struggles occurring in Japan with those on the Asian mainland, and as far as the Iberian Peninsula, to a universal antifascist struggle.

Following a crackdown on leftist organizations in Nara in August of 1932, Hasegawa was arrested on the suspicion of harboring "dangerous thoughts" (*kiken shisō*), a code for any display of leftist activity that ran contrary to the national polity. Earlier that summer she and her classmate Nagato Yasu had begun meeting and corresponding with local unionists and communists, including Ōyama Shunpō and Fujimoto Tadayoshi, who were all too eager for the two women's help with their organizing efforts in Nara, where 95 percent of the region's textile workers were women.[8] Although neither Hasegawa nor Nagato were arrested during the infamous August 31 sweep—they were both staying with their respective families during the summer vacation—the police apprehended them on their return to school in September. As recalled by classmate Mizuno Hamako:

> It happened one night in 1932, on the 9th of September, after the students had all returned to the dormitory from summer vacation. In any event, we were just settling back into dormitory life when Hasegawa and Nagato were arrested by the police and did not return to school.

Translator's Introduction   5

All of us who'd returned from Hokkaidō, Korea, Kyūshū and elsewhere had brought out our souvenirs, and all the rooms were bustling with activity. It was a hot, humid night, and the side of our room facing the hallway was covered by a bamboo screen. All of a sudden, from inside the room, I saw men in white uniforms pass through the dark hallway, swords jangling at their waists. At first, I thought that there'd been an outbreak of some infectious disease. But a moment later, the men in white returned, followed by five or six girls walking with tense footsteps. The girls were roommates of Nagato, who was being arrested, and had come to see her off. We later heard that the two of them [i.e., Nagato and Hasegawa] were "reds." No other explanation was needed in those days.[9]

After a week-long stint in jail, Hasegawa was expelled from college, returning to her parents' home by the year's end.

Unfazed by her arrest and expulsion from college, Hasegawa joined the Japanese Union of Proletarian Esperantists in 1933 and, for the next few years, committed herself to the global Esperanto movement. She volunteered as a typist at the Japanese Esperanto Institute, attended various Esperanto meetups in Tokyo, and contributed fiction, drama, criticism, and translations to domestic Esperanto magazines like *La revuo orienta* and *Esperanta literaturo,* as well as to international ones like *Infanoj sur tutmondo,* an Esperanto magazine for children. In February 1935 she and her sister formed an Esperanto reading group called the Klara Circle (Klara Rondo), named after Klara Zamenhof, the wife of the language's inventor, and the German activist Clara Zetkin, which they ran out of their parents' home, much to the annoyance of their rightist father.

That same month the Klara Circle was contacted by Ye Laishi, a Chinese Esperantist looking for contributions to a Women's Day issue of his magazine, *La mondo,* published out of Shanghai. Hasegawa responded to Ye with an article titled "Women

6 Translator's Introduction

Workers in Wartime Japan" in which she ridiculed the misogyny of Japan's state ideology, decried the gross pay imbalances among men and women workers, demanded safer and more supportive work environments, and urged women to mobilize against militarism at home and abroad. Signing her article Verda Majo, Esperanto for "Green May," Hasegawa expressed her allegiance to both the Esperanto and proletarian movements.

Sometime in early 1936, Hasegawa met and fell in love with a Chinese exchange student and fellow Esperantist by the name of Liu Ren. Liu hailed from the Japanese puppet state of Manchukuo and, like many young Chinese progressives of his day, had found in Esperanto a linguistic safe space for internationalists to collaborate against fascism. In autumn of that year, Hasegawa married Liu against her parents' wishes and the conventionally racist "concerns" of her friends. In addition to being an act of love, Hasegawa believed her marriage to be an act of international solidarity and antifascism, as she would later note in her autobiography: "For Esperantists like myself, nationality is not something absolute. If anything, it signifies only a difference of language, custom and culture.... To date, hundreds if not thousands of Japanese women have crossed that trench to marry Chinese men. Whether their paths have been florid or thorny, I cannot say. All that I know is that their love is at once international and personal. I too am one such woman. Where I differ is in the fact that my love is inseparable from my Esperantist beliefs."[10]

Early in 1937, Liu returned to China to join the burgeoning anti-Japanese invasion movement there. Hasegawa followed a few months later, helped by some of Liu's friends (who were subsequently arrested for assisting her). Of course, she was not alone in heading to China in order to freely express, in word and action, her resistance to Japanese militarism. Other Japanese leftists, notably Kaji Wataru and Ikeda Yuki, also saw the free port of Shanghai as a strategic base of operations for waging ideological warfare beyond the reach of their home's increasingly expansive police state.[11]

Not every self-professed progressive or radical showed such daring in the face of injustice. Indeed, Hasegawa's uncompromising commitment to transnational solidarity made her stand out among her peers. In this respect the journalist, educator, and anarchist Mochizuki Yuriko serves as an interesting foil. Both women espoused leftist ideas that connected women's liberation to the liberation of humanity, and Mochizuki's interest in the internationalist Bahá'í religion even connected her for a time with Esperantists like the blind anarchist storyteller Vasily Eroshenko. Furthermore, both women left Japan in the 1930s, in part so they could find the freedom to disseminate their ideas and ideals outside the constraints of wartime censorship laws. That said, Hasegawa and Mochizuki quickly diverged, both geographically and ideologically, the former relocating to besieged Shanghai to participate in the anti-invasion movement via Esperanto propaganda and the latter relocating to colonial Manchuria, where she began promoting various state-sponsored discourses of Japanese superiority in order to justify the building of agrarian communes there.[12] Although Hasegawa never called Mochizuki out personally, she pointed a proverbial finger in numerous writings at former "comrades" for ideologically converting from the Left to the Right in order to gain or maintain influence or for falling silent to avoid punishment. Uncompromising in her antifascist, Esperantic humanism, Hasegawa was no hypocrite.

On April 19 she arrived in Shanghai, and for the next half year, semiconfined to the second floor of a drab apartment in the French Concession, she learned a bitter lesson. She had come to Shanghai looking to participate in the anti-Japanese resistance but spoke not a word of Chinese. Moreover, she could not move about freely lest the discovery of her ethnicity result in deportation or, worse, a revenge attack. It is one thing to want to contribute to a cause; it is another to find one's proper place in it. "My first and all-important task," she later recalled from the heart of Fighting China, "was to become accustomed to my circumstances as quickly as possible and to learn to communicate."[13] Thanks to

8 Translator's Introduction

Esperanto, this urgent need to "communicate" came easily, in a sense.

Writing for the Italian weekly *Il grido del popolo* in 1918, the Marxist thinker Antonio Gramsci had once criticized Esperanto as a "cosmopolitan," not an "internationalist," medium of communication for "the bourgeois who travels for business or pleasure."[14] While this may have been true prior to the establishment of expressly political Esperanto organizations like the Sennacieca Asocio Tutmonda in 1921, a distinctly proletarian, a-/ internationalist, and anti-imperialist Esperanto movement flourished throughout the midcentury. As noted by Edwin Michielsen, a historian of transnationalist activism in East Asia, "Gramsci failed to take into consideration the existence of multi-ethnic and multilingual empires and socialist states...where Esperanto could be useful to support interlingual communication."[15] Moreover, in countries like China and Spain, which witnessed antifascist/ anti-imperialist wars in the 1930s, Esperanto helped to mediate not only between different language groups *within* these countries (for example, between speakers of Spanish and Catalan in Spain and between Mandarin and Cantonese in China) but also among internationalists who joined their struggles from abroad. "Why is it that I, a Japanese woman, find myself thinking about you, a Spanish general?" Hasegawa would later write to Julio Mangada, a prominent Spanish Republican Army officer. "Is it love? Yes, if by love is meant the green love of Esperanto."[16]

Although Hasegawa was committed to learning Chinese, knowledge of the international language no doubt helped her to integrate quickly with progressive circles in Shanghai. Besides, she already had one friend in the city, Ye Laishi, with whom she had corresponded two years prior. Through Ye and his Esperanto comrades, Hasegawa began taking part in events put on by the Chinese Proletarian Esperantist Union and the Shanghai Esperantist League and writing for the internationally distributed Esperanto journal *Ĉinio hurlas*. As her network grew and grew, she became increasingly comfortable appearing in public, boldly choosing to march in an anti-Japanese demonstration in June 1937.

But there was little time to get settled. Hasegawa had arrived on the eve of the Lugou Bridge Incident, the start of Japan's full-scale invasion, and on August 13 she witnessed the Battle of Shanghai. When Shanghai fell in November 1937, Hasegawa and Liu made plans to flee to Hankou, the center of the Chinese resistance.

The journey would not be easy. They would not only have to avoid security checks at sea, gunfire on the ground, and air strikes from the sky but would need to carefully tread the gauntlet of a smoldering civil war between two factions of the Chinese resistance, the revolutionary Chinese Communist Party (CCP) and the nationalist Kuomintang (KMT). Since 1923 the CCP and the KMT had agreed to two short-lived fronts to resist Japanese aggression, each time betrayed by the latter's power-hungry leader Chiang Kai-shek. While a second front was agreed to in 1937, lasting until the end of the war, tensions remained high throughout, each side eyeing the other with suspicion.

In December, Hasegawa and Liu arrived in Guangzhou, where they were once again obliged to go into hiding upon learning that the KMT had issued a decree calling for the immediate dissolution of interracial marriages between Chinese and Japanese nationals. While the young couple waited patiently to secure safe passage to the more liberal city of Hankou, they formed connections with Cantonese Esperantists, many of whom were young and eager students at Sun Yat-sen University. Although they helped to establish an Esperanto division in the KMT's propaganda department, the discovery of Hasegawa's Japanese identity resulted in her deportation to Hong Kong at the start of the new year. Upon arriving in Guangzhou, Liu had appealed to the high-ranking official and poet Guo Moruo, then head of the Third Bureau of the Ministry of Political Affairs, to safeguard against such an outcome. But as bureaucrats are wont to do, even if they be "poets," Guo merely expressed his sympathy with the noncommittal exclamation "A tragedy!"[17]

One can hardly imagine how painful this deportation order was for Hasegawa. She was not only separated from her husband; the KMT's charge threatened to isolate her from the very people for whom she had forsaken hearth and home. Unfortunately, there is no record of what Hasegawa did during her four-month exile in Hong Kong. She could have gone back to Japan and sought refuge with friends but chose not to. Not for the last time did her conviction about the great moral injustice being done to China urge her to stand firm. Fortunately, Liu arrived in July with word that he and Ye Laishi had at last convinced Guo Moruo to secure Hasegawa's passage to Hankou, where the Central Propaganda Department was in need of a Japanese speaker for its radio division.

Hasegawa's stay in Hankou was short but significant: "How brief but exciting, invigorating but tiring it was!"[18] A world-renowned symbol of antifascism, Hankou was unique in its tolerance of political freedom, attracting tens of thousands of refugees of all political stripes.[19] In addition to broadcasting anti-Japanese propaganda over the radio, Hasegawa attended resistance events, made impassioned appeals to Esperantists worldwide, and began writing under the Chinese name Luchuan Yingzi.

When Hankou fell in October 1938, Hasegawa and Liu fled to Chongqing, the new wartime capital, which she described in bleak terms as being "covered by a dense fog."[20] As relations between the CCP and the KMT continued to deteriorate, it grew increasingly difficult for progressives to work with the nationalist government, especially in Chongqing, which was under the political control of Chiang Kai-shek's secret police chief, Dai Li. Nevertheless, Hasegawa continued her radio work for the Central Propaganda Department, joined Kaji Wataru's Japanese People's Anti-War Alliance, and made new friends, including the writer Xiao Hong and the Korean Esperantist An Useng, who lived in

China between the years 1919 and 1945. An Useng was the nephew of An Chunggŭn, a member of the Korean independence movement who shot and killed former Japanese prime minister Ito Hirobumi at a railway station in Harbin on October 26, 1909.

Besides being a political activist, An Useng was a poet and translator using the Esperanto pseudonym Elpin. He is well-known for his contributions to an Esperanto translation of the collected works of Lu Xun. His poem *The Dove of Peace*, included in this book before the translations, was dedicated to Hasegawa and has appeared in both of her collected works and her translated works.

Although it is difficult to gauge exactly what impact Hasegawa's propaganda had on the front lines in China, so impassioned were her speeches that Miyanishi Naoki, a signal officer in the Japanese army, wrote down the following words in a poem upon catching one of her broadcasts: "Radio Chongqing—I secretly listen to the eloquent Japanese words, unable to sit still."[21]

Hasegawa's radio work made her a hero in China. At the same time, it outed her identity to Japanese agents, who publicly labeled her a "sweet-voiced traitor" (*kyōsei baikokudo*) and went so far as to advertise her family's address in national newspapers.[22] However, being labeled a traitor did not cause Hasegawa to waver in her resolve. Rather, in an open letter to Japanese Esperantists, she responded defiantly to the scandal, criticized what she saw as her compatriots' lack of humanity, and called out the self-proclaimed Left for their silence and/or cooperation with Japan's fascist regime:

> Call me a traitor, if you wish! I am not afraid. Rather, I am ashamed to belong to a nation that has not only invaded another, but is carelessly creating a living hell for innocent and helpless refugees. True patriotism does not stand in the way of mankind's evolution. If it did, it would be chauvinism. And how many chauvinists has the war

12   Translator's Introduction

produced in Japan! I could scarcely hold back my anger and disgust when I heard how intellectuals who had once claimed to be conscious, progressive, and even Marxist, are now shamelessly following reactionary militarists and politicians, beating the drum for "the just cause" of the Imperial Army.[23]

In 1941 Hasegawa published an Esperanto translation of Ishikawa Tatsuzō's *Ikiteiru heitai* (Soldiers Alive) and a collection of writings titled *Flustr' el uragano* (A Whisper from a Storm). In October of this same year, she gave birth to a son, Xing. In 1944 she began writing a memoir of her experiences in China, *En Ĉinio batalanta* (Inside Fighting China).[24] Although she managed to write and publish a third of the work, frequent disruptions and worsening health caused her to abandon the project.

The longest work in this collection, *Inside Fighting China* is also Hasegawa's most celebrated. Although technically "incomplete," it offers a fascinating glimpse into how one antiwar activist practiced the ideals she preached and the obstacles she faced to do so. For a wartime autobiography, it contains few descriptions of battles, and much wandering, but importantly, it showcases the banal suffering of the displaced, against which Hasegawa occasionally, and in full honesty, interrogates her own middle-class privilege. Written in an engaging mix of present and past "tenses" (which, although a common feature of Japanese, I have decided to consolidate for the most part into a single past-tense narrative for the sake of clarity), it is full of fresh insights into how Japanese nationals, women, refugees, and internationalists from all over China endured this turbulent and bloody time in Chinese history. As once observed by Parks Coble, "It is clear that there is no one, no master narrative of this experience [i.e., the Sino-Japanese War]."[25] As such, a microhistory like *Inside Fighting China* offers us a fascinating glimpse into one of countless experiences that a more sweeping macrohistory might ignore.

After the war ended, Hasegawa and her family departed

for Liu's home in Northwest China. However, renewed fighting between the CCP and the KMT shattered any hope of a return to normalcy. In 1946 she gave birth to a daughter, Xiaolan, and, toward the end of the year, relocated to Harbin, where she and Liu found work on the Editing Committee of the Northeast Administrative Council before moving to Jiamusi. When she became pregnant a third time in January 1947, she decided to get an abortion, owing to the physical and psychological toll imposed by continual conflict. The procedure, performed under unsanitary conditions, was not a success, and she consequently contracted an infection and died at the age of thirty-five. Liu is said to have stayed by her coffin for an entire month, dying of kidney failure in April of the same year.[26] Afterward, their children were cared for by the local government as "orphans of revolutionary heroes."

While Hasegawa lived to see the end of Japan's invasion of China, she remained to the end skeptical of its ruling elite, whose capitulation to the Allied forces she described in her 1945 essay "Japan at a Crossroads" as mere self-preservation, "not owing to the fact that its military strength was exhausted, or that it felt compassion for its people" but "because its ruling elite wanted to preserve as much of its power as possible."[27] As she saw it, in "conveniently discarding their old warrior garb and donning the costume of peace and democracy," Japan's war criminals would seek a new collaboration—now with the anticommunist United States. Ever an incisive critic of high ideals, she declared: "We are not asking for a Japan built on anti-Bolshevism. We want a democratic Japan."[28]

Had Hasegawa lived to see the proclamation of the People's Republic of China in 1949, one wonders, would she have eyed it with the same skepticism? After all, she was an Esperantist first. Despite her communist sympathies, she was suspicious of ideological dogmatism, as she had suffered for it herself and knew how ideology could be twisted to various ends—just as Esperanto had been twisted by some in Japan to serve the state's colonial agenda. Surely, she would have welcomed the arrival of the People's

14 Translator's Introduction

Republic as the overturning of an old social, political, and economic order at a time when the world was in need of reckoning with the underlying causes that had unleashed the horrors of the Second World War. But what would she have made of the CCP's disastrous Anti-Rightist Campaign, the Great Leap Forward, and the Cultural Revolution, all of which were ideologically "justified" yet significantly damaging to democracy in China? Perhaps the decisive role played by the CCP in fighting the Japanese army and offering an alternative to capitalist hegemony would have hardened her commitment to the party. Then again, her Esperantism may well have pushed her to abandon party politics altogether, as was the case with Miyamoto Masao, the Esperanto poet and one of Hasegawa's future translator-cum-biographers.

Thanks to the efforts of Chinese and Japanese Esperantists like Ye Laishi, Takasugi Ichirō, and Tone Kōichi (Yoshida Susugu, pseud.), in the two decades following Hasegawa's death a Japanese translation of *Inside Fighting China,* as well as *Teru no shōgai,* a biography, was published, though primarily circulated among Esperanto and left-wing circles. A chapter dedicated to her was also included in Ōshima Yoshio and Miyamoto Masao's 1974 *Hantaisei esuperanto undōshi,* a history of antiauthoritarian activism among Japanese Esperantists. However, it was not until the 1980s that interest in her life story became widespread in both Japan and China. One catalyst for this was an effort made by Hasegawa's children in the late 1970s to establish contact with their Japanese family, a story that received significant news coverage. Another and perhaps more important catalyst came in the diplomatic thaw between Japan and China, during which various attempts were made to promote stories of international friendship that might symbolize close ties between the two nations.[29] Naturally, one such story was that of Hasegawa Teru, whose life was given a soapy retelling in the television drama *Bokyō no hoshi,* the first coproduced by Japanese and Chinese networks. The popularity of *Bokyō no hoshi* coincided with the publication of two more translations of her selected works and more biographies.

Decades later when *Agora,* a Tokyo-based antiwar feminist journal, published three special issues on Hasegawa Teru between 1999 and 2004, several contributors cited the television drama, and not her actual writings, as their starting point for learning about her inspiring human rights activism.

What impact has a romanticized retelling of Hasegawa's life had on the reception of her political ideas in the public sphere? The historian Erik Esselstrom has observed that "whereas Hasegawa's understanding of the struggle for human rights during the 1930s and 1940s intertwined social, economic, gender, and political conflicts, her postwar admirers embrace in large part only her pacifism."[30] Focusing on the intersection of politics and gender, the anthropologist Hideko Mitsui has suggested that contemporary Japanese women tend to be impressed with how Hasegawa's life must have been "an exciting adventure from traditional family obligations and the thrills of international romance."[31] Could these reductions of Hasegawa to "pacifist" and "romantic cosmopolitan" be the result of her popularization through the commercial medium of television? Concerned by what they see as a narrow discursive frame through which Hasegawa's life is currently understood, Esselstrom and Mitsui point to a loss of nuance in her legacy.

While there is truth to Mitsui's and Esselstrom's respective arguments that the complexity of Hasegawa's politics has been circumscribed over time, I think there is something unfair in suggesting that contemporary Japanese audiences, and especially Japanese women, have an unnuanced or romanticized view of her life and ideas.[32] That Hasegawa's name has been invoked in the domestic contexts of remilitarization and women's rights and in the international contexts of Vietnam, Afghanistan, and Ukraine shows that her legacy remains vitally connected to a meaningful network of sociopolitical discourses, both national and international.[33] Therefore, while I agree that Hasegawa's legacy may at times be circumscribed, particularly within the context of preserving Article 9 of the 1946 Japanese Constitution (by which Japan

16 Translator's Introduction

renounces "war as a sovereign right of the nation"), and that there is a need to fully appreciate her life for its breadth and depth of activism, as is the case of all activists whose stories have been filtered through overly commercial media, I am perhaps less cynical in my assessment of the degree of critical thinking being done by those individuals who encounter Hasegawa's life story, be it in a book or on television, and are inspired by it.[34] Among the admirers of Hasegawa with whom I have corresponded are anarchists, communists, liberals, and self-described "apolitical pacifists" who are well capable of drawing a line from her sociopolitical views to such extranational issues as the Russian army's invasion of Ukraine, the State of Israel's occupation of Palestine, the global refugee crisis, modern forms of political and corporate imperialism, and the continued injustices being wrought against Indigenous Peoples across the Americas. Surely, anybody who has been curious enough to learn more about Hasegawa by way of Takasugi Ichirō's 1980 biography, *Chūgoku no midori no hoshi,* has been stirred by its final imperative: "Teru's life-story seems to be shouting desperately towards the future: 'Internationalism must be protected like the apple of the eye. To this end, let us oppose military aggression, no matter what country it stems from, nor how "noble" the pretext under which it is carried out. May we never again repeat [the Lugou Bridge Incident of] July 7.' "[35]

Hasegawa's literary influence, too, arrived long after her passing. This should come as no surprise. After all, she only published a handful of writings in Esperanto before leaving Japan for China, and it is likely that few of her writings while there made it back due to wartime censorship. Not to mention, by the time *Inside Fighting China* and *A Whisper from a Storm* finally became available to most Japanese Esperantists, McCarthyism and Cold War fearmongering had caused left-wing literature to fall somewhat out of fashion.[36] However, as interest in Hasegawa's life story developed in the mid-1970s and early 1980s, this situation began to change, and Esperantists worldwide were among the first to recognize her literary talent. Perhaps Hasegawa's greatest influence has been on the internationally translated Croatian author and Esperantist Spomenka Štimec, who wrote a play about Hasegawa in 1986 and whose 1993 novel *Kroata milita noktlibro* (Croatian War Nocturnal) is moved by a spirit of optimism amid tragedy that is reminiscent of *Inside Fighting China*.[37] More recently, Hasegawa has inspired young, award-winning Japanese authors like Aonami An and Kobayashi Erika (an Esperantist herself), both of whom are drawn to the literary drama of her life as well as to her courage and resolute commitment to internationalism.[38]

The writings of Hasegawa Teru are valuable for the clear yet complex ways in which they articulate the various feminist, pacifist, and antifascist beliefs that circulated the globe in the early and mid-twentieth century. They will hopefully contribute to the growing body of historical literature on transnational cooperation currently being written by Sho Konishi, Ian Rapley, Edwin Michielsen, John Sexton, Brigid O'Keeffe, Jordi Martí-Rueda, and others. Moreover, as rightly noted by Mitsui, an interest in Hasegawa's life and ideas may help with "diversifying the ownership of cosmopolitanism and feminism and decenter the [Eurocentric] assumptions we tend to impose on [them]."[39] This is more important than ever, as the so-called West (that fictional political entity defined and upheld by a collective racist imagination) postures as the sole "defender" of human rights despite its complicity in and indifference to such rights abuses at home and abroad.

Last, it is my hope that this work will contribute to an expanded understanding of Esperanto, which Konishi has described in his illuminating *Anarchist Modernity*, a study of ideational exchanges between Japanese and Russian intellectuals at the turn of the twentieth century, as a "nongovernmental movement (NGM) rather than a nongovernmental organization (NGO)," developed at a grassroots level without "the cultural imperialism embedded in the organizational composition of many of the existing international NGOs of the day."[40] Today, popular understandings of Esperanto tend to dismiss the language as a quasi-NGO and novelty language that never really broke from its

18 Translator's Introduction

Eurocentrism. There is truth to this claim. Moreover, the movement has largely turned inward, increasingly prioritizing linguistic refinement and the creation of an Esperanto identity over transnational projects of political significance. However, as demonstrated by Konishi, Michielsen, and Rapley, Esperanto also has a rich history as an interpeople's language in Eastern Europe and Asia, where it once allowed for the exchange of radical ideas in a medium designed to be a transnational gesture of solidarity. While I am not suggesting that the Esperanto project need be taken up again, I do think it is worth reevaluating such a creative (if flawed) means for transcending the various barriers that keep people apart.

Returning to the Liu Ren quotation at the beginning of this book, the writings of Hasegawa Teru are indeed "a memento from the ordinary life of an ordinary woman," albeit a most extraordinary one. Surely, Hasegawa was aware of the extraordinary potential latent within all people, including herself: how, with the proper motivating force, anybody can find a sense of purpose beyond the ordinary self, unlocking a vast network of cooperative action. For her this motivating force was no doubt Esperanto, as she observed at the outset of *Inside Fighting China:* "One month ago, I turned twenty-five. If an average life-span be fifty years, I have passed over half of it. The first half was very ordinary, and the next promises nothing extraordinary. For I am an ordinary woman. And yet I believe that I can do bigger and more significant things in China than I would have been able to do in Japan. For I am an Esperantist." To those unaware, the meaning of "Esperanto" is "one who hopes." And hope, it sometimes seems, is increasingly absent from our world, as I imagine it must have appeared in the mid-twentieth century. As I write this, our world burns from searing wildfires, capitalism continues to impoverish the many while enriching the few, the invasion of Ukraine drags on for yet another year, the Far Right tightens its grip on the disaffected of Europe, and the IDF reduces Gaza to rubble while world leaders look the other way (and not for the first time). It has become increasingly difficult to find hope anywhere. And yet it is there, ever growing, among extraordinary "ordinary" people; outside the traditional institutions of power; in grassroots organizing for the disenfranchised; at protests against racial and identity-based hatred; at labor strikes for humane treatment and deserved pay; in arts groups seeking to build communities, not donors; in quality independent journalism. As in all dark periods of our collective history, there are people who hope—for a better world not for themselves, nor their nation, nor even humankind but for all the living, breathing earth.

Per laboro de la esperantoj!
(By the labor of those who hope!)

Although a great admirer of Hasegawa's life and ideas, the translator Miyamoto Masao has suggested that her literary talent is "of an immature class when compared to the output of her contemporaries."[41] Considering the lack of polish in her writing, the abundance of grammatical errors, and the occasional use of tired tropes, one can see why. However, I personally share the sentiments of the German critic Klaus Schubert, who pointed out that "[Hasegawa] wrote in an idiomatically rich, non-European, and creative Esperanto."[42] As I have always preferred naive, nonconforming creativity to shallow eloquence, I think there is something fresh and exciting about the way Hasegawa articulated certain ideas in a young language that she herself had only just learned. While I have sought to make her writing more legible in English, I hope that I have also been able to preserve its unique charm.

With respect to the various Esperanto nom de plumes and abbreviated names in the original text of *Inside Fighting China*, I have opted to use each historical figure's actual name, where possible, for the sake of clarity. To this end, I am deeply grateful to the work of Ye Laishi and Miyamoto Masao, both of whom supplied this information in Hasegawa's collected works and later in her translated selected works.

Having little knowledge of Chinese, I was regrettably

20 Translator's Introduction

unable to trace Hasegawa's work written under her Chinese pen name Luchuan Yingzi, with the exception of her final essay, "Japan at a Crossroads," which I translated from Shibata Iwao's Japanese translation of the Chinese "original." Readers may note that this essay lacks the clarity found in Hasegawa's other pieces, which I believe indicates that the original may in fact have been written first in Esperanto and then translated into Chinese, making my own a translation of a translation of a translation.

Last, while I could have included some of Hasegawa's Japanese and Esperanto fiction, I decided that this collection was not the best setting to showcase such works. That said, I look forward to future contributions from translators and scholars and am willing to share any archival sources I have encountered in my research.

Notes

1. Nishimura Yukiko, "Teru ni tsuite," in *Hasegawa teru sakuhinshū: Hansen Esuperanchisuto,* ed. Miyamoto Masao (Tokyo: Nihon tosho sentā, 1994), p. 203.

2. Ibid., p. 205. The short story "Spring Madness" (Printempa frenezo) is narrated by a psychologically unstable high school student who, seized by a sudden desire to see her family, runs away from school, only to be met with coldness, criticism, and shame from her parents. The story culminates in the recounting of a suicide attempt. Hasegawa Teru, "Printempa frenezo," *Esperanto bungaku,* May–June 1934.

3. Ĵelezo (Ye Laishi), "Pri Verda Majo," in *Verkoj de Verda Majo* (Beijing: Ĉina Esperanto-Eldonejo, 1982), p. 1.

4. Yamada Yukiko, "Kōhai Hasegawa Teru," in Miyamoto, *Hasegawa teru sakuhinshū,* p. 203.

5. L. L. Zamenhof, quoted in *Esperanto: Language, Literature, and Community,* ed. Humphry Tonkin, trans. Humphry Tonkin, Jane Edwards, and Karen Johnson-Weiner (Albany: State University of New York Press, 1993), p. 23.

6. Ibid., p. 35.

7. Hiromi Sasamoto-Collins has put forth a convincing justification for applying the term "fascism" to prewar and wartime Japan. See "Facilitating Fascism? The Japanese Peace Preservation Act and the Role of the Judiciary," in *Fascism and Criminal Law: History, Theory, Continuity*, ed. Stephen Skinner (Oxford: Hart, 2015), pp. 163–189.

8. Miyamoto Masao and Ōshima Yoshio, *Historio de La Kontraŭreĝima Esperanto-Movado/Hantaisei esuperanto undō-shi* (Tokyo: Sanseidō, 1987), pp. 258–259.

9. Mizuno Hamako, quoted in ibid., p. 261.

10. Verda Majo, *Verkoj*, pp. 28–29.

11. Erik Esselstrom, "The Life and Memory of Hasegawa Teru: Contextualizing Human Rights, Trans/Nationalism, and the Antiwar Movement in Modern Japan," *Radical History Review* 101 (Spring 2008): pp. 148–149.

12. Tatsuya Kageki has written an illuminating essay on Mochizuki's ideological conversion. See "An Anarchist Woman's Ideological Conversion: How Mochizuki Yuriko Became a Nationalist in Manchuria," in *Women in Asia under the Japanese Empire*, ed. Jiajia Yang and Tatsuya Kageki (New York: Routledge, 2023), pp. 134–148.

13. Majo, *Verkoj*, p. 36.

14. Quoted in Peter Ives, *Language and Hegemony in Gramsci* (London: Pluto Press, 2004), p. 56.

15. Edwin Michielsen, "Assembling Solidarity: Proletarian Arts and Internationalism in East Asia" (PhD diss., University of Toronto, 2021), p. 135.

16. Majo, *Verkoj*, p. 409.

17. Ibid., p. 86.

18. Ibid., p. 105.

19. John Sexton, *Red Friends: Internationalists in China's Struggle for Liberation* (London: Verso, 2023), p. 255.

20. Majo, *Verkoj*, p. 106.

21. Quoted in Xinli Zhao, "Nitchūsensō-ki ni okeru Chūgoku-kyōsantō no tainichi puropaganda senjutsu senryaku: Nipponhei horyo taiō ni miru '2-bu-hō' no imi" (PhD diss., Waseda University, 2010), p. 104.

22. For example, "Kyōsei baikokudo no shōtai ha kore," *Miyako shinbun*, November 1, 1938, p. 13.

23. Majo, *Verkoj*, p. 378.

24. The title may have been a play on "France combattante" (Fighting France), the name used by the political entity that claimed to be the legitimate government of France between the years 1942 and 1944.

25. Parks M. Coble, *China's War Reporters: The Legacy of Resistance against Japan* (Cambridge, MA: Harvard University Press, 2015), p. 103.

26. Hasegawa Akiko, "Watashi nari no heiwa no ayumi," *Yami wo terasu senko: Hasegawa Teru to musume Akiko, Agora* 253 (October 10, 1999): 87.

27. Quoted in Esselstrom, "Life and Memory of Hasegawa Teru," p. 153.

28. Ibid., pp. 153–154.

29. For a good overview of the media cooperation between Japan and China following the two countries' realignment of official relations in 1972, see Stephanie DeBoer, *Coproducing Asia: Locating Japanese-Chinese Regional Film and Media* (Minneapolis: University of Minnesota Press, 2014), pp. 85–86.

30. Esselstrom, "Life and Memory of Hasegawa Teru," p. 155.

31. Hideko Mitsui, "Longing for the Other: Traitors' Cosmopolitanism," *Social Anthropology* 18, no. 4 (2010): 414.

32. Esselstrom, "Life and Memory of Hasegawa Teru," p. 156.

33. Ibid., p. 155; Sexton, *Red Friends,* p. 261; *Verda Majo Tsūshin,* no. 38 (October 25, 2022).

34. Constitution of Japan, chapter 2, article 9, Prime Minister's Office of Japan, July 16, 2023, https://japan.kantei.go.jp/constitution_and_government_of_japan/constitution_e.html.

35. Ichirō Takasugi, *Chūgoku no midori no hoshi* (Tokyo: Asahi shinbun shuppan, 1980), p. 198. The same can be said of Miyamoto Masao's introduction to Hasegawa's selected works, which quotes from Marx and Lenin: "I imagine that what Teru wanted to say to us can be summed up by the following words: Workers of the world, unite! Workers of the world and oppressed peoples, unite!" Miyamoto, "Hasegawa Teru no shōgai to sono jidai—hensha maegaki," in Miyamoto, *Hasegawa teru sakuhinshū,* p. 21.

36. Heather Bown-Struyk and Normal Field, introduction to *For Dignity, Justice and Revolution: An Anthology of Japanese Proletarian Literature,* ed. Heather Bown-Struyk and Normal Field (Chicago: University of Chicago Press, 2016), p. 7.

37. Alessandra Madella, "On 'Hodler in Mostar'—an Interview with Spomenka Štimec," ESF Connected, July 16, 2023, https://esfconnected.org/2022/08/29/on-hodler-in-mostar/.

38. "Shōsetsu Subaru shinjinshō jushō 'yanfa no uta' kankō kinen Aonami An 'katararenai rekishi ya hitobito o tan'nen ni kaku koto,'" Shueisha Bungei Station, January 2, 2025, https://www.bungei.shueisha.co.jp/interview/yanfa-2/.

39. Mitsui, "Longing for the Other," p. 414.

40. Sho Konishi, *Anarchist Modernity: Cooperatism and Japanese-Russian Intellectual Relations in Modern Japan* (Cambridge, MA: Harvard University Press, 2013), p. 26.

41. Miyamoto, "Hensha no atogaki," in Miyamoto, *Hasegawa teru sakuhinshū,* p. 269.

42. Klaus Schubert, "Arda batalo por libero," *Esperanto* 935, no. 11 (November 1983): 192.

THE DOVE OF PEACE

Elpin

> To Verda Majo, a Japanese Esperantist
> broadcasting for a Chinese radio station.

In an eastern land made mad by war,
You, a lamb before wolves and serpents,
Bravely fought to reckon all.
Having formed at heart a righteous plan,
You forsook your home,
Your parents, friends, and flew to foreign shores
With firm resolve: to give to those you left behind
A life of peace ever fit for man.

Now, a prophet with a microphone, you speak
Truth to your compatriots.
Your voice, gentle, yet fully capable
Of making thunder. Wise words you dedicate
To souls whose consciences are clear.
Your voice will not resound in vain,
But will surely rend asunder
The heart by blood enthralled, the cause of pain.

The Dove of Peace 25

But what is it we hope from you, dear friend?
O dove of peace from just across the sea!
You did not merely spring your cage
But with the ardent fire of youth
Refused to rest inert 'neath cherry-blossom trees,
Your soul deprived of all but apathy.
O *May,* make *verdant* these fields so dark and gray[1]
Before the coming of the autumn harvest!

---

1. "O May, make verdant…": a pun on Hasegawa's Esperanto name, Verda Majo, which translates to "Green May."

Part 1

INSIDE FIGHTING CHINA

1

INSIDE FIGHTING CHINA

> What time is shorter
> than the passing spring?
> What sorrow, longer
> than the parting of friends?
>
> —Shimazaki Tōson

A Late-Spring Farewell

The port of Yokohama is bustling with noise.

A whistle shrieks, signaling my ship's imminent departure.

Between ship and shore play colorful waves of countless streamers. But my hands are empty, holding nothing to tie me to the tearful well-wishers below. Am I really leaving my homeland as lonesome as an autumn leaf blown by the wind?

Suddenly, I catch the words of a song from the bubbling din on the shore: "A new feeling has come into the world; through the world a mighty call is passing...."[1] It is clearly being sung by

---

Epigraph: Shimazaki Tōson (1872–1943) was the pen name of Shimazaki Haruki, a writer who was active in the Romantic and Naturalist genres during the Meiji, Taisho, and early Showa periods. The quotation is from the first stanza of his poem "Banshun no betsuri," which shares the same title as Hasegawa's first chapter ("A Late-Spring Farewell").

1. Here and in the following quotation, Hasegawa quotes from the first and last two lines of the poem "La espero" (The hope), written by L. L. Zamenhof, the inventor of Esperanto. "La espero" is considered by many to be the unofficial anthem of the universal language.

a small crowd of Chinese comrades who helped me to secure my undocumented passage to China, and with whom I will reunite soon enough.

I sing along in my heart.

The ship lurches forward, as if sliding from the face of the earth. For a brief moment, the colorful streamers all appear to be fixed in space before scattering at once over the ocean like so many fallen blossoms. The singing on the shore is now becoming more and more muffled: "Till mankind's beautiful dream of eternal fortune is realized..." Soon I can no longer hear my friends as they wave their white handkerchiefs in a sign of farewell. The gulf between the ship and shore is growing wider by the minute and the crowd smaller and smaller. Though my eyes remain fixed on my friends, I know that I am not looking at them but at something else, something invisible....

I stand tense, motionless.

Far, far away is the land on which I, for the past twenty-five years, have woven pink dreams, red tempers, black malaises, and green loves.[2]

I watch it slowly pale to gray.

Oh, let it not become a grave for everything I have forsaken!

The ship begins to pick up speed, threshing white waves in its wake. The blue sea is still and calm; the azure sky, serene.

It is the middle of April 1937.

I am sitting quietly on my cot in the steerage of a great British ship. Seated around me are some dozen men, women, and children, all of them Chinese. *Chinese*—yesterday they would have been mere

---

2. Many references to the color green can be found in this and other Esperanto works. In addition to symbolizing hope, green is often used synonymously with "Esperanto" or "Esperantist." The green star (*verda stelo*) was first proposed as a unifying symbol for Esperantists in 1892.

foreigners to me, but today they are my travel companions, and tomorrow, they will be my compatriots.

Many Japanese dislike the Chinese and look down on them as lesser beings. In their minds, the Chinese are enduringly symbolized by the queue, which they say resembles a pig's tail. Even when they meet a Chinese person in modern European dress, they claim to catch the odor of garlic and lard, which seems to trigger in them an almost instinctual repulsion. But what do they really know about the Chinese? To be sure, they know that the Chinese abhor the Japanese and fight them everywhere, often resulting in much bloodshed. So it is no wonder that my parents and relatives chide and reproach me for actively trying to bring "shame"—*their* word, not mine—upon myself and my family by my marriage to a Chinese man. At the same time, regarding my journey to Shanghai, they are all on edge, as if I were throwing myself into a mob of bloodthirsty enemies.

My close friend assures me that she knows the young people of China are entirely different from their Japanese counterparts, the majority of whom have neither work ethic, hope, nor passion and only vegetate like old men. Indeed, she tells me that she understands my love but adds that, if she were me, she would resign such love, lest it throw my one-and-only mother into the depths of utter despair. The day before my departure, this friend of mine sent me a short letter, in which she wrote: "I cannot come to see you off. Only on paper am I brave enough to say goodbye. So goodbye, dear friend. Be happy, and don't forget me. Should things not work out in the end, I want you to know that you can always come home, where I will prepare a room especially for you."

My friend uses words like "know" and "understand." But in reality, she knows and understands little. For her, China is so very far away.

Meanwhile, for Esperantists like myself, nationality is not something absolute. If anything, it signifies only a difference of language, custom, and culture. We see each other, rather, as belonging to one great "human race." Not in some vague, theoretical sense, mind you—we *feel* it, intensely. And while outwardly, we are connected by one universal language, inwardly, we are connected by one universal feeling. Of course, we also love our own nations. However, our love is one that necessarily stands shoulder to shoulder with the love and respect owed to all other nations.

Right now, in Germany, Hitler is promoting ideas of racial superiority and purity in his aim to sow hatred among his people for the other races of Europe. He is the common enemy of Esperantists in every nation of the world, including Germany. The same can be said about the Japanese government, whose elites have strived to dig a trench between the Japanese and Chinese peoples, one that they are continuously striving to make deeper and wider, to give the impression that it is both natural and uncrossable.

To date, hundreds if not thousands of Japanese women have crossed that trench to marry Chinese men. Whether their paths have been florid or thorny, I cannot say. All that I know is that their love is at once international and personal. I, too, am one such woman. Where I differ is in the fact that my love is inseparable from my Esperantist beliefs. And so, for better or worse, my future will be somewhat different from theirs.

In Shanghai, I am awaited by my husband, who arrived there sometime before me. Aside from him, I have no one else. Similarly, for him, a citizen of a remote northeastern province, Shanghai is an entirely foreign city. But this does not cause me to waver. I say that "I have no one there." But that is not really true. For I will surely find *green* friends there, Chinese Esperantists, although I do not know their names yet.

One month ago, I turned twenty-five. If an average life span be fifty years, I have passed over half of it. The first half was very ordinary, and the next promises nothing extraordinary. For I am an ordinary woman. And yet I believe that I can do bigger and more significant things in China than I would have been able to do in Japan.

For I am an Esperantist.

Rocked by the waves, the ship rocks my heart.
We are now at sea.

"Think no more!" I tell myself. "Above all else, you must arrive safely in Shanghai. And may nothing happen to you on the way!"

On the second night of my voyage, the ship stops outside the port of Nagasaki, the last Japanese port on the route to China.[3] We stop for one hour, one long and nerve-wracking hour. I let out a sigh when at last the whistle blows.

On the iron-plated deck, a cool evening wind fondles my hair. The port lies far in the distance. Behind it, Nagasaki appears all lit up like a beautiful fairy-tale castle. The lights are blinking, as if signaling to me a thousand wondrous tales. But am I still the sort of little girl who is drawn to such charming and childish things?

Before me lies the free ocean, separating me from my homeland and loved ones. At the same time, it is leading me to a new life and new friends.

Goodbye, my homeland! Goodbye, dear friends!

Tonight, in my dreams, I will watch the softly falling cherry blossoms and, between them, catch sight of the round black eyes of my only niece.

Shanghai

Laborers and Skyscrapers

Although more than six years have passed, I can still vividly recall the moment I disembarked in Shanghai and found Ren waving to

---

3. According to Miyamoto Masao, Hasegawa is omitting the fact that the ship also docked in Kobe, during which time she paid a visit to her brother-in-law, the Esperanto poet Nishimura Masao, and Kusuri Kei, a communist Esperantist. The omission, like others in this work, was likely made to protect people's identities. See Miyamoto, *Hasegawa Teru sakuhin-shū*, p. 97fn3.

me from the bustling crowd.[4] To call what I felt then "joy" would be inaccurate. It was more complicated. I silently took his hand in mine, lacking the words to express myself. For some strange reason, it seemed that his hand had grown larger and warmer than I remembered it.

At noon, on the nineteenth of April, 1937, I took my first step on Chinese soil. As I was to spend the next half year living in Shanghai—until the war was to drive us south—one might expect it to have left a favorable impression on me, that it had been a most memorable city. But to tell the truth, I did not like it at all.

The first thing I saw on disembarking was a crowd of half-naked laborers toiling beneath serried rows of modern architecture. The contrast so strongly affected me that, years later, whenever I hear the word "Shanghai," I reflexively conjure up these starkly opposing images. I suppose that it is the origin of my dislike for Shanghai.

The skyscrapers had been built, story by story, by the sweat and blood of those half-naked men. And no sooner had they finished their labor than they were sent back to earth, to crawl about like beasts, while their foreign-born masters delighted in everything indispensable to civilized life, including a myriad of special pleasures forbidden in their homelands. Indeed, Shanghai is the Paradise of Adventurers.[5] And such adventurers do not give so much as a thought to the dirty, half-naked men who build their towers. Between the one and the other, there is no direct line of communication. Instead, the orders of master to slave are conveyed by way of "high-ranking" Chinese who can babble on in foreign tongues or by the blunt cudgels of hired Vietnamese and Sikh police officers.

By the time I had arrived in Shanghai, the sign in front of

---

4. Liu Ren (?–1947): An Esperantist and the husband of Hasegawa Teru. He is referred to simply as L in the original.

5. A reference to a popular guidebook of the time. G. E. Miller [Mauricio Fresco, pseud.], *Shanghai, the Paradise of Adventurers* (New York: Orsay, 1937).

the public garden bearing the words "Dogs and Chinese Not Admitted" had already been removed, but the situation remained unchanged: the laborers never appeared in such places. Even in the third-class compartments of trams exclusively reserved for Chinese people, they were nowhere to be found. No matter how civilized and modern Shanghai may appear, working people there still lead rather primitive lives. During the day, they pull rickshaws and carry heavy loads, doing what in their masters' nations is done by machines or livestock. Their houses—mere straw huts—serve them only for a stony sleep, be it for the night or for all eternity. And all of them have colorless, sunburnt faces. Not only do they not understand the languages of their masters, but they also cannot read or write their own. Therefore, if their master says yes, they fear a beating, and if they say no, they fear arrest. So they do not dare to learn the difference, for they are not looked upon as human beings, not in life nor in death. And if they die on the street from hunger, disease, or the cold—which is not altogether rare—people simply get rid of their corpses as if they were those of stray dogs.

To be sure, Shanghai is a "special" city, one with many distinguishing characteristics. And indeed, it appears to be a great world's fair, exhibiting people of every race, each living their own distinct life. But aside from the contrast of half-naked laborers set against a backdrop of luxurious skyscrapers, I feel there is really nothing that can better reveal the true nature of Shanghai: a typical city of semicolonized China.

So no, I do not like Shanghai. For it brings to mind the image of a dismembered body, and that image is simply too painful for me to bear.

Confined to the Second Floor

After staying with an old friend of Ren's for a few days, we rented two small rooms in the French Concession with a married couple whom Ren had known in Tokyo. As the rooms shared a single entryway, our friends agreed to live in front, to spare me any uncomfortable encounters with meddlesome strangers.

Our one-window room was dark and unfurnished. The walls, perhaps once white, were splotched yellow and gray. Occupied by only two trunks, a handbag, a typewriter, and a small bed, the room seemed vast, drab, and cold.

Ren and his friends came up with the following story for me: "Mrs. Liu was born in Malaya and is returning to China for the first time, where she has family. However, she only understands the Malay tongue (what we called Esperanto)."

Fortunately, the concession was not Tokyo. Here, nobody cared about your identity or career. Not the landlord, not the neighbors, not the police.

I had to start everything from scratch. The woman we were boarding with became my teacher. Every morning, she went out to buy food while I, the lowly apprentice, washed dishes. I soon learned to start a fire—in modern Shanghai, most Chinese do not have gas stoves!—and later to cook. We only ate twice daily, at noon and at night, to save money. Naturally, we ate "Chinese food," though not the kind that is famously eaten all over the world. Rather, we ate that other kind, made from cheap vegetables cooked in soybean oil and seasoned with salt, and occasionally served with a bit of meat.

Everyone jokingly called Ren "the luckiest man in the world," for he lived in a European apartment, kept a Chinese diet, and had a Japanese wife.

How false were his treasures!

Our unfortunate "lucky man" and his friend worked at a newly founded publishing house that printed pamphlets on current affairs. Its editor in chief was a respected journalist by the name of Yuan Zhu, who happened to have returned from Japan on the same ship as Ren, with whom he had also shared a cabin. He was short and stout and gave the impression that his small body was a boundless mass of energy. Personally, I found him to be intelligent, deft, resilient, and nimble. Although his publications suggested that he was of the progressive camp, nobody quite knew what he really thought or did. Some claimed that he was sympathetic to the Communist Party, while others argued just the opposite. After the fall of Shanghai, he chose to stay on in the city. Some believed that he was doing underground work, while others said that he had long been communicating with the enemy. Later, we learned from a Japanese newspaper article that he had taken up an important post in the Shanghai puppet government. Even today, few believe him to have been a mere collaborator. An enigmatic man indeed. I saw him a few times. He spoke Japanese rather well. After the Shanghai Incident, when his publishing house went under due to a loss of financial support, he paid me a sudden visit.[6] Perhaps he knew that I was home alone at the time. I remember that he wore black sunglasses and Chinese clothes, which was unusual for him. During our short conversation, he casually asked me where my family lived, how they were faring, and whether Ren had any friends or relatives in Tokyo. Sensing that something was wrong, I tried to answer him as vaguely as possible. That was the last I saw of him.

My teacher-friend was unemployed but often went out on various errands. During such times, I stayed in, reading Chinese or Esperanto books or playing with the landlady's two stepdaughters. As we later discovered, the landlord had lived in Nagasaki for several years, where he had married a Japanese woman who bore him a girl and died. Upon his return to Shanghai, he married a Chinese woman who bore him two boys. For some reason, he hung a large portrait of his dead Japanese wife in the most conspicuous spot of his front hall. Later still—after we had moved—we learned that he was in fact a "collaborator" and had been killed on his way home from his "office." One of my little playmates, both of whom

---

6. Shanghai Incident: A reference to the Battle of Shanghai, the first of many engagements between the National Revolutionary Army of China and the Imperial Army of Japan. Lasting from August 13, 1937, to November 26, 1937, it signaled the start of China's War of Resistance.

were twelve years old, was the daughter of the landlord's Japanese wife, while the other was the orphaned child of his relative. Because they were unhappy children, we all became fast friends, despite our linguistic barrier. The little half-Japanese girl remembered nothing of her mother and seemed unwilling to talk about her. But one time I happened to find her staring fixedly at the photo in the front hall when nobody else was around. My little friend told me that her stepmother often called her a "little devil" in her father's absence.

My first and all-important task was to become accustomed to my circumstances as quickly as possible and to learn to communicate—that is, to "become Chinese." Otherwise, we would have to hide forever in the small French Concession.

Imagine, for a moment, that you have suddenly become mute and deaf. All around you, everybody is living just as vigorously as they were before, but you are alone among them. You do not understand them, nor they you....

I thought that I had prepared for this temporary feeling of alienation, but thought does not necessarily obey reality. Oddly enough, I felt it most intensely when we were with friends. They all spoke so happily, with laughter and excitement. Meanwhile, I strained to capture their racing words and invariably grew tired, unable to listen anymore. Then I would bow my head and stare silently at the floor. At such times, it seemed to me that even Ren, who was laughing with the others and getting excited about something incomprehensible to me, was no longer mine but someone foreign, distant....

Then one day in the middle of my second month in China, Ren and his friends were talking over lunch: "The days are getting longer. Two meals are no longer enough to live on." "Yeah, I wake up so hungry." "Let's eat in the mornings, then." "Bread will do." "Nah—too expensive. Let's make congee instead."

"I—I understood that!" I cried, like a child, and repeated the words that they had just spoken.

"So you did!" they cried back with delight.

Owing to our poor financial situation, neither bread nor congee ever materialized. Nevertheless, I was pleased with myself. For the first time, I had understood a few full phrases of rapid Chinese conversation, word for word.

Before leaving Japan, I had promised the editor of a progressive literary magazine that I would send him reportage or translations from Shanghai.[7] This promise I could not fulfill right away. I only translated one article, "How Did the Flowers Bloom?," about the night before the Xi'an Incident.[8] The writer appeared to have served in the army of General Zhang Xueliang, one of the chief actors in the epoch-making drama. I submitted my translation under a Chinese pseudonym to *Nihon hyōron*, a Tokyo monthly with a considerably large circulation. After several weeks, I received a copy of the issue carrying my translation, a fifty-yen money order and a letter from the editor in chief, Murofuse Kōshin. He had taken me for a Chinese youth and asked me to continue submitting translations of the same sort. Ren received the money at the Bank of Japan on August 12, and the very next day, the Japanese army shelled the city. Had we been late by one day! That fifty-yen payment, obtained just in the nick of time, served us well during the difficult days that followed.

The first few months passed over quickly. It was a new life for me, but prosaic and often tedious. Travelers to foreign lands love to wander streets like schooners at sea, encountering no familiar face, but I was deprived of even this pleasure. The famous

---

7. Miyamoto suggests that the editor may have been Kishi Yamaji or Maruyama Yoshiji, both of whom worked for the proletarian magazine *Bungaku annai*. Of course, Hasegawa could merely be referring to Murofuse Kōshin, mentioned soon after. See Miyamoto, *Hasegawa Teru sakuhinshū*, p. 97fn6.

8. Xi'an Incident: A political crisis that took place in late 1936, when Chiang Kai-shek, the leader of the nationalist Kuomintang government, was detained by his subordinate generals Zhang Xueliang and Yang Hucheng. They forced him to ally with his political rivals, the Chinese Communist Party, in a unified front against the Japanese Empire's growing invasion of China.

bright lights of Shanghai were another world to me, a poor undocumented immigrant. In addition to being estranged from modern living, I was also cut off from the earth itself: I lived on the second floor, with neither garden nor flowerpot. On occasion, I traded my wooden floors for asphalt streets, visited friends, or went on short walks, only to return to my drab, half-lit room. In the course of this routine, I forgot the pleasant feeling of the soft, fresh earth. Had I not been an Esperantist, and unable to breathe the green air of universal solidarity, my life then would surely have been colder and more suffocating.

Beneath the Green Star

One day during my first week in China, two men knocked at our door. One of them entered stiffly, with long strides, while the other entered with short, quick steps that shook his whole body. The first man was tall and broad-shouldered, with eyes that stared in one direction behind his thick glasses and who was as still as a statue when he spoke. The second man looked shorter and narrow-shouldered, with eyes that wandered constantly. Without opening his mouth, he seemed to be snickering.

These two very dissimilar youths did not vex me with flowing, incomprehensible Chinese, nor with stilted, broken Japanese.

For they were Esperantists like me.

"Do you know this comrade from Tokyo?" asked the tall man, whose name was Ye Laishi, as he took out a notebook.[9] "We corresponded before."

"Hah!" I exclaimed, for there on the page was written my Japanese name and address. "I should say that I know her well," I continued. "It's me!"

We all broke out in a peal of laughter.

---

9. Ye Laishi (1911–1994): An Esperantist and editor of various Esperanto magazines, including *La mondo, Ĉinio hurlas*, and *Heroldo de Ĉinio*. He collected and translated Hasegawa's works after her death. His Esperanto nom de plume, Ĵelezo, comes from the Russian word for "iron" (железо).

I recalled how a few years prior I had contributed an article to the monthly Esperanto magazine *La mondo,* published in Shanghai, and, on one or two occasions, had corresponded with its editor in chief. Well, now he was speaking with me!

During the course of our conversation, it became clear that Ye had also corresponded with Ren when he was in Beijing. So this prominent member of the Esperanto and Latinxua movements in China was not a new friend at all, but an old one for us both.[10] Later, during our most difficult days of the war, he would become a benefactor in various senses of the word. I do not know how we will ever thank him enough.

"People say that I look Japanese," said the other comrade, whose name was Zhang Qicheng, bowing at the waist.[11] "What do you think?"

At the time, Zhang was working at an engineering firm, but in the second year of the war, he left to become a journalist for the *Xinhua ribao,* the most progressive paper in the country, and set off for Singapore. Then, after the Japanese Imperial Army extended its talons there, he was arrested by the British authorities, who mistakenly took him for a Japanese soldier. As for what happened to him after the surrender of the island, we are not entirely sure. Some say that he eventually managed to escape his captors and is now working somewhere near Shanghai. Oh, may that be true!

As I mentioned before, Ye and Zhang, who jokingly called each other Bull and Mouse, were perfect opposites at first glance. However, the serious-looking Ye was often very

---

10. Latinxua movement: The Latinxua Sinwenz (Latinized New Script) movement was an effort initiated in Russia, in the late 1920s, to create a means for rapidly increasingly literacy in China. The movement was supported by intellectuals like Guo Moruo and Lu Xun.

11. Zhang Qicheng (1912–2004): An Esperantist and editor of various Esperanto magazines, including *La mondo* and *Ĉinio hurlas.* In 1951, after the foundation of the People's Republic, he helped form the Chinese Esperanto League and edited its organ *El popola Ĉinio.*

humorous, while the humorous-looking Zhang was often a serious-minded worker. Neither man had more than thirty years at the time.

Youthful, earnest, and progressive—such are the common traits of Chinese Esperantists. Indeed, I have never met among them a "graybeard," nor a dandy—wanting only to chat, sing, and go chasing after girls—nor a hypocrite, nor a chauvinist. Unlike in Japan, in China I do not need to consider the politics or the social status of my interlocutor. For here, everybody is a comrade or friend of the same standing.

The Shanghai Esperanto League (SEL), the center of the Esperanto movement in China, was located on a side street in the British Concession. On the ground floor was an Esperanto Bookstore, which, despite its name, consisted of but a few shelves and above it, a meeting hall. In the adjoining rooms lived Yue Jiaxuan, the president of the SEL, together with his wife and three children, the eldest of whom was a ten-year-old boy capable of speaking a smattering of Esperanto. Now, if this description leads you to assume that Yue was a dull middle-aged man, you'd be dead wrong. Why, at the time, he was hardly thirty years old! A youth like the others, then, thanks to whom the SEL gave off a more intimate and warm impression, as if it were not merely a simple office space.

Unfortunately, Yue's loving family, like countless others, has since split up because of the war. And yet, with indefatigable optimism, he continues to work with us for the movement in the heart of Free China, while his wife and little ones live far away, in their Japanese-occupied birthplace. His eldest is now well into his teens, fighting in some warzone for one of the most courageous resistance armies.[12]

On the fifteenth of July, under the aegis of the SEL, we

---

12. Hasegawa may be referring to the New Fourth Army, a unit of the National Revolutionary Army that was uniquely under the direction of the Chinese Communist Party.

celebrated the fiftieth anniversary of the invention of Esperanto with more than three hundred kindred spirits, new and old. Representatives from Guangzhou, Beijing, and other cities also attended. We sincerely criticized our work up to then and fervently took counsel regarding the work to come. It was the week after the Lugou Bridge Incident, and the excitement and unease of the outside world permeated our green gathering.[13] Nobody knew for certain how the situation would develop nor whether our program would be realized or not. At the same time, nobody felt at heart a contradiction in being a Chinese citizen and an Esperantist. In China, Esperanto is used not for disseminating scientific reports to the world, nor for facilitating the international sale of commercial goods, nor for hosting foreign tourists, and certainly not for fascist propaganda. The ideals of Esperantists and the Chinese people are one and the same: to be neither the oppressed nor the oppressor. For a long time now, Chinese Esperantists have flown high the flag on which is written: "For China via Esperanto!"

At the congress, some three hundred voices united to recite "La espero" and "Tagiĝo," besides many a passionate song of freedom:[14]

> Arise, ye people who refuse to be slaves!
> With our flesh and blood, let us build a new Great
>   Wall![15]

---

13. The Lugou Bridge Incident, also known as the Marco Polo Bridge Incident, a battle fought during July 1937 between China's National Revolutionary Army and the Imperial Japanese Army. It is generally regarded as the start of Japan's full-scale invasion of China.

14. As mentioned earlier, "La espero" is a poem by Zamenhof. "Tagiĝo" (Dawn) is a poem by Antoni Grabowski, a Polish chemical engineer and Esperanto writer.

15. From "March of the Volunteers," a patriotic song from 1934 and 1935 with lyrics written by Tian Han and set to a melody by Nie Er. It has been the official national anthem of the People's Republic of China since 1978.

Fight back to our old home, fight back to our old home!
Drive away the Japanese Empire, the Northeast is ours![16]

The congress finished in perfect harmony and with great enthusiasm. Each person shook hands with the other, warmly exchanging parting words of *ĝis revido* (until next time). In ordinary days, they would see each other a day, a week, or, at most, a few months later. Indeed, at the very least, on the fifteenth of December, on Zamenhof Day, they would again gather under the green star of Esperanto. But who among them supposed that they would not see each other for several years? Already two or three months following the celebratory gathering, they began to drift: some went to Hankou and later to Chongqing, following the government; others took up arms, throwing themselves into the army or guerilla outfits, or ran northwest under the red star of communism; still others returned to their hometowns or cities for work and bread; and the rest stayed in Shanghai. When would they reunite? Perhaps there would be one or two people whose hands they would never hold again...who would give their lives to the nation. However, I believe that none of those three hundred attendees could honestly endure the temporary peace of Wang Jingwei's puppet government.[17] Such would have been entirely impossible for Chinese Esperantists.

Today, when it is difficult for even thirty Esperantists to come together, I recall, with a heavy heart, that congress and think about its more than three hundred attendees, though I did not know the majority of them personally.

Incidentally, I am also reminded of two comrades who had helped me secure safe passage to China and who were still in Tokyo at the time of the congress. Prior to the outbreak of the Lugou

---

16. From "Fight Back to Our Old Home," a patriotic anti-Japanese song from 1936 with lyrics written by An E. and set to a melody by Ren Guang.

17. Wang Jingwei (1883–1944): A Chinese politician who sided with the Japanese Empire in 1940 to form a collaborationist government in Nanjing.

Bridge Incident, the Japanese government had made a mass arrest of progressive Chinese student-activists. Among the arrestees were two men by the names of Deng Keqiang and Huang Yihuan.[18] They were charged for conspiring to send a Japanese Esperantist to the All-China Esperanto Congress mentioned above, organized by the Comintern in Moscow. If the Esperantist in question was in fact myself, I must beg a thousand pardons of them, especially of Deng, who later, in his native province of Guangdong, had to experience the bitter taste of incarceration for my sake.

The first person to notify us of the arrest was Huang himself. He wrote in late June, saying: "Deng was arrested last week, and I will be taken in tomorrow or the day after. But fear not—things may not be as bad as they seem."

And that is just what happened.

The deceased fathers of both men had been famous revolutionaries who had dedicated much of their lives to helping found the Republic of China. Huang's father had fled to Tokyo with Sun Yat-sen when the 1911 Revolution failed and there befriended Tōyama Mitsuru, now the leader of a fascist group.[19] Apparently, because Tōyama explained to the superintendent general of the Tokyo Metropolitan Police that Huang was a "personal friend," he was soon released. Returning to Shanghai, he came to us straightaway and reported: "The torture that Deng had to endure was so terrible that it somewhat messed with his head. The devil knows when they will let him go...."

A quiet and studious youth, Huang later moved to Yan'an,

---

18. Deng Keqiang (1912–1944): The son of revolutionary Deng Naiyan, he learned Esperanto under Nakagaki Kojirō, a pioneer of Japan's proletarian Esperanto movement, while studying at Meiji University in Tokyo. His Esperanto nom de plume was Dinko. Huang Yihuan (1917–2004): The son of Huang Xing, the first commander in chief of the Republic of China. His Esperanto nom de plume was "Ivano."

19. Hasegawa may be referring to the Kokuryūkai (Black Dragon Society) or the Genyōsha (Black Ocean Society), both ultranationalist groups at one time headed by Mitsuru.

where life is completely different from that of our own. Only once did we receive a letter from him, in which he wrote that he was working and studying hard, had served in the army, and was now happier and more active than any of his old friends could imagine. We also saw his works in some Esperanto magazines that occasionally reached us.

Thanks to my Esperanto friends, Shanghai was not at all a foreign city for me. In truth, none of us had a particularly good handle on our common language, which, while unfortunate, did not strike me as being terribly important. Sometimes I would go for a walk near the SEL with Comrade I. She would speak to me in Chinese, and I to her in Esperanto. From our talks, I gathered that she was the daughter of an important gentry family, a situation that engendered all kinds of angst in her. I never quite knew how many of my words she really understood. But we always spoke to each other intimately, with excitement, as we walked up and down the street, not ever wanting to part.

Comrade L., a nineteen-year-old girl, had previously been employed at a textile mill but was fired for taking part in a strike. Afterward, she moved in with her Esperantist boyfriend. He gave her six yuan a month for living expenses, for he himself earned very little teaching workers at a night school. To live on six yuan a month! How difficult, even if the price of goods was not so high. She confessed to me that she could not even afford the minimum nutrients to support her health. However, she was always happy and talkative. She once explained to me excitedly, in a torrent of words, not suspecting that I might not understand her Shanghainese dialect, how the Japanese capitalists were exploiting and tormenting the Chinese workers. Later, she found work at a large publishing house, which paid her sixteen yuan a month. At the end of the month, she came to me beaming and said: "Today it'll be *me* who treats *you* to lunch!" And grabbing my hand, she took me out to a small but clean restaurant, where we each had a bowl of fried noodles and duck congee. When it was time to settle up, she bent down and, from her right stocking, withdrew a ten-yuan note, which she proudly put in our waiter's hand. I do not know how much change she received. I only felt sorry she had to sweat so much for my sake. But she was very happy, and I was happy for her.

It is difficult for Chinese and Japanese workers alike to master Esperanto, first because of the low level of their education, and second because of the disparity between Esperanto and their national tongues. Furthermore, in China, young, intelligent workers tend to throw themselves into the maelstrom of pressing social struggles rather than stand back beneath the green star of Esperanto. Therefore, we should not hold it against our Chinese comrades that their skill in the language is relatively poor.

On August 13, Shanghai, which was already on edge from the Lugou Bridge Incident, was shaken directly by shelling. And together with the bombs, the citizens, including us Esperantists, exploded with rage:

"Down with Japanese imperialism!"

"Liberate China!"

"Freedom for China via Esperanto!"

Despite various difficulties, a dozen experienced, long-standing comrades effectively revived the magazine *Ĉinio hurlas*, which had ceased to appear but a couple of years prior.[20] The first issue was duplicated with a jellygraph; the second was printed. And the third, you ask? Hah, the military situation was far too urgent by then!

I wrote for this publication, transcribed its manuscripts, and corrected its printing errors. As I expressed at the time in my article "Victory for China Is the Key to Tomorrow for All of Asia": "My work with *Ĉinio hurlas* and other such magazines is not confined to contributing my miserable technique as a foreign Esperantist to help produce some flimsy rag. Whenever I take up

---

20. The name *Ĉinio hurlas* (China roars) may have been a nod to *Roar, China!* a 1926 play by Sergei Tretyakov.

my pen, my blood boils at the oppression of justice, and a fiery rage is stoked against the brutish enemy. I rejoice: I am with the Chinese people!"

Thanks to Esperanto, I was neither a total foreigner in Shanghai, nor did I feel like a passive observer of the war, even though, at the time, I could not publicly take part in the Chinese resistance against the Japanese aggressors.

The War as Seen from the Safety Zone

An Indignant Song Breaks Out

Under bright lights, men were getting drunk on sweet brandy, their arms wrapped around their women's waists, singing "Oh, my rose!," and "I love you, my dove!" Meanwhile, another sad and stirring melody was making mute that debaucherous strain as it resonated throughout the streets, penetrating the human heart.

April's evening breezes were arousing bittersweet thoughts in the breasts of migrants while perhaps more bittersweet still were the thoughts of exiles from the northeast provinces beyond the Great Wall.

> Since the great catastrophe began,
> We have suffered rape and looting.
> Bearing this hardship, we fled elsewhere.
> Away from us, our parents died.[21]

> This was followed by another song, decisive and brave:
> Fight back to our old home, fight back to our old home!
> Drive away the Japanese Empire, the Northeast is ours![22]

---

21. From "The Great Wall Ballad," a patriotic anti-Japanese song from 1937 with lyrics by Pan Jienong and set to music by Liu Xue'an. It was written after the Lugou Bridge Incident.

22. From "Fight Back to Our Old Home." See note 16 for details.

Then it was May. On either side of the quiet streets in the French Concession, acacias wore fresh leaves of green and wafted the fragrance of their snow-white blossoms. However, at heart, their blossoms were red. Blood red.

> May flowers bloom in the fields,
> Over the blood of the patriots.
> In order to save our perilous nation,
> They fought to the very end.[23]

But it was not only those people from beyond the Great Wall who were singing. By now most Chinese people were well aware of the fact that the Manchurian Incident was not a mere thing of the past, that it had been the first step taken by the aggressor against the Republic of China, and that tomorrow, even, a similar "incident" might take place right above their heads. Melodies pregnant with real feeling rushed, skipped, and flew from one street corner to the next, all over the city of Shanghai.[24]

The Xi'an Incident, which occurred on December 12 of the previous year, had dealt a decisive blow to the pro-Japanese forces in government, functioning as a sort of "railroad switch" for national politics in general.

But the light of day did not arrive so smoothly, or swiftly. A great darkness continued to reign for a long time over China.

One day in June, the streets of the International Settlement took on an appearance different from that of ordinary days. Men were

---

23. From "May Flowers," a patriotic anti-Japanese song from 1936 with lyrics by Guang Weiran and set to music by Yan Shushi.
24. Manchurian Incident: Also known as the Mukden Incident. On September 18, 1931, the Japanese Imperial Army staged a false-flag event as a pretext for invading Northeast China, during which Chiang Kai-shek ordered the Northeastern Army to retreat south beyond the Great Wall of China.

walking in groups of two, three, and five—it was not clear from where, but they seemed to be walking in the same direction. Then, little by little, they came together, like several streams converging as a river—an unstoppable torrent flowing from one street to the next, crying in one thunderous chorus:

> With our flesh and blood, let us build a new Great Wall!
> The Chinese people face their greatest peril.
> From each person comes forth the urgent call to action.
> Arise! Arise! Arise![25]

> From time to time, a collective cry was raised.
> "Down with Japanese imperialism!"
> "Free our leaders!"

The cries were coming from a protest demanding the liberation of "the Seven Gentlemen."[26] These six men and one woman were neither communists nor radicals but bourgeois liberals—writers, lawyers, and bankers of comparatively high social status. They were imprisoned simply for founding a popular, nonpartisan anti-Japanese organization in Shanghai, one that the people themselves had greatly desired....

As they marched on, the protestors sang and cried, their voices thundering as one, voices until now divided and suppressed.

And I was there with them, my arms linked firmly with those of my friends. It is possible that I was the sole foreigner, the only Japanese, among them. And if I was? I, too, had the right and duty to demand the freedom of Chinese patriots. My heart beat with theirs; my blood boiled as theirs did. It was only the sounds

---

25. From "March of the Volunteers." See note 15 for details.

26. The Seven Gentlemen: A group of seven intellectuals (one of whom, Shi Liang, was a woman) who were arrested in 1936 by Chiang Kai-shek's government for collaborating with the CCP in the national salvation movement against the Japanese invasion. The nonpartisan anti-Japanese organization referred to hereafter was the National Salvation Association.

from our mouths that were different, though I, too, moved my mouth while they sang their songs:

> We are millions with but one heart,
> Braving the enemy's fire, march on!
> Braving the enemy's fire, march on!
> March on! March on, and on![27]

In spite of the policeman's saber, the protesters marched on, tasting for themselves the yet unripe fruit of the Xi'an Incident.

War Breaks Out—to No One's Surprise

June 7—

Cannons thundered, shaking the air outside the ancient capital of Beijing. Even in Shanghai, people could hear it, their hearts racing. Would the shelling continue, or would it cease immediately? As usual, the Japanese repeated, like trained parrots, that they did not want the fighting to spread. For their part, the people of Shanghai hoped that the flame of China's resistance would not go out, its sliver of freedom buried once again in ashes. At the same time, they feared that a great catastrophe could descend on them at any moment.

And their hope and fear arrived together.

August 13—

A fateful day. A day etched in blood. It happened so suddenly, but was it really unexpected? Not at all. War never starts on the day that it breaks out. Indeed, it is as Clausewitz, the author of *On War*, writes, simply "politics by other means." While the Japanese fascists proclaimed that they had to thoroughly and at all costs punish the Chinese people for being anti-Japanese in thought and action, the living facts spoke for themselves. Had we

---

27. From "March of the Volunteers." See the note 15 for details.

all really forgotten about the Manchurian Incident from only a few years back? And extending our gaze even further back, were the painful experiences of the past sixty years somehow not sufficient to open our eyes to the truth?

"Lies written in ink cannot disguise facts written in blood."

"Blood debts must be repaid in kind."[28]

The war had at last broken out—but to no one's surprise. It was bound to happen sooner or later.

And now it was here.

Nowhere to Go

"Hello? I've been told that a Japanese woman lives here."

One day we were surprised to hear the voice of a woman speaking Japanese outside our apartment door.

Ren and his friends glanced at me before rushing over to investigate.

"There's no such person here. Perhaps you misheard."

"Certainly not," said the woman, raising her voice. "I know that she's here." Then, lowering her voice again, she added: "I live on this street. Nearly all the Japanese in Shanghai have gone home, and tomorrow, the last ship will depart. I want to board it but can't do it alone. Would she not come with me?"

She sounded so pitiful.

"I'm sorry, ma'am, but you're speaking to the wrong people. There's no Japanese woman here. Besides, I'm sure you'll be fine. Once you get on board, you'll find other Japanese people. Now go—it's not safe here."

The woman dared not speak more. Though I did not see what she looked like, I imagined her leaving with a bowed head and a heavy heart.

She did not appear again before us, and we ourselves moved two days later. I know not whether she left on that ship.

---

28. Two phrases coined by the writer Lu Xun.

Perhaps she did, like most other Japanese wives. As was the case with the Manchurian Incident in 1931 and the first Shanghai Incident in 1932, these women had to leave their husbands to temporarily ensure their comfort and safety. In either case, they had been able to return to China, and the arms of their husbands, a few months after things had settled down. But what about this time? Even if everything went as before, their lives would be constantly under threat of newly imposed barriers. Their unions, therefore, could not be perfect. For even on bright, sunny days, some disquieting force full of contradiction must have thrown a black cloud over them.

Homeland! Bewitching word! Surely those who had a homeland to return to were happier than I, who could neither go home nor enter my husband's, obliged to wander the "Safety Zone" like a hare at bay.

The French Concession was not only a Safety Zone for me, a Japanese woman in Chinese dress. Well before the cannons thundered in Zhabei, a procession of automobiles with mountains of objects piled on top of them had made their way here one after the other. And waiting for them with sly smiles were landladies who were most often White Russian émigrés. There exists in this world no law that protects such émigrés, nor one that punishes them. Money is their almighty law. They happily raised rents and evicted tenants to welcome the more "well-heeled refugees."

"Excuse me, miss," our White Russian landlady said to me one day while I was washing clothes. "Don't you send your clothes to the laundries?"

"Oh no. I wash them myself. I suppose I must have too much free time," I replied, stretching the limit of my English vocabulary.

"I see. Well, the reason I'm asking is that our water supply is limited enough as it is, and the utility fees are climbing higher...."

I knew that this was an excuse. But what could we do? We had moved into the room of a friend about to leave for the interior. After he left there would still be ten days of the month for which he had paid. While we would be blessed with a similar opportunity later on, this time we were obliged to pay for the rest of the week, and at a higher price than our friend had paid. Perhaps this was to be expected in a time of war.

In any event, we paid up.

At the month's end, to appease our landlady, we took out twenty-five yuan from our threadbare wallet to give to the landlord's Chinese servant.

His face was stiff as a wooden mask.

"The master says his relatives are arriving from Zhabei and has decided that..."

"Come now, brother," Ren interjected, patting the servant on the shoulder and sliding the bills into his hand. "This is a time of national crisis."

The man went away and returned shortly after, extending to us his open right hand.

They wanted *fifty yuan* now? My god! Twenty-five was already too much for this unemployed couple to spare. We had one hundred yuan in total, half of which had come from my translations, for which I had been paid the day before. We definitely needed to rent a room but could live without bread?

Bloodsuckers! We didn't argue. Our first duty was to live, and for that we had to conserve something more important than bread and board.

We went out to look for a room. A room? We already knew that our search would be in vain. Our hearts were heavy with leaden despair. A gray rain was falling outside. Aimlessly, we walked the streets, now forward, now to the side, now back. Every street was overflowing with refugees. They were refugees in the true sense of the word, for the "well-heeled" refugees had already found comfortable shelters for themselves. They were now likely smacking their lips on European delicacies, drinking coffee, and going out to the movies and dance halls. With automobiles, they carried objects both necessary and superfluous, as we had seen. But the others had nothing, aside from their bedding and clothes, though some had not even that. For them, the most they could do was carry themselves on their two legs. One barefoot, middle-aged woman with a vacant stare walked carrying only an empty sauce jar. Surely, she herself was not conscious of why she had saved it from the enemy cannon fire and was now carrying it as if it were her sole treasure. One could say that these people were blessed, for in spite of everything they had found themselves in the Safety Zone. Could they not see how countless other people were bawling and shouting outside the now-shut iron gates of the concession, begging the guards to let them in? The concession was a Safety Zone for both middle- and lower-class refugees. Indeed, here no bullets nor bombs would reach them. Yesterday was like a nightmare. But was this place really so "safe" for them? Some of these people, whose strength was spent, crouched by the road half-dead. And the rest kept going, knowing not where, and we went with them....

"Good woman, kind sir!"

Again and again, hands appeared before me—withered, callused, childlike.

"Have pity on me. I haven't eaten anything in three days."

I gave a wry smile. It was no wonder that they saw me as wealthy. I was wearing brand-new clothes. (Where would I have bought a worn-out Chinese dress?) But what difference was there between us and them? If only they knew that we, too, had not eaten since the morning and had no bed to sleep in for the night.

Time and again, a chill ran through me. What if they were to recognize my race? As things stood, nobody had the right to ask of them a reason for distinguishing friends from enemies among the Japanese. I went on, nerves shot, trying to imitate the bearing of a Shanghainese woman.

And gray was the drizzling rain.

The air was cold for the middle of August. Colder still were our hearts and theirs. We wandered with them, street after street, aimlessly, hopelessly, listlessly. However, the red fire within me never went out. Did the spilled blood and tears of their countrymen not make it burn within them even more passionately?

By late afternoon, we had dragged ourselves to the SEL. From his lofty place on the wall, Dr. Zamenhof looked down on us through his round spectacles, with gentle and compassionate eyes. But what could he offer us? Had he not died tragically under the cannon fire of the First World War? Ah, but from his disciples there appeared a savior—Comrade Feng, a poet, whom we had never met before. He said that he had two rooms and that he would give us one of them.

Infernal Cries Swirl Outside

A Mexican writer once described the Japanese as a fearful race of demon lords.[29] While some people say that their soldiers act like wild beasts, others insist that their cruelty only makes them worse.

A Japanese myself, I will not contest these sentiments. But they do seem to be a bit redundant. The Japanese are in fact fascist aggressors. Does such a description not suffice? Why dress this up in figurative language?

During the day, from our balcony, we watched two active volcanoes endlessly spouting plumes of smoke, covering the blue sky black. At night, those places turned a hellish red. Long, fiery tongues thrust themselves into the air.

But they were not real volcanoes. They were Zhabei and Nanshi. From the air, the Japanese were hurling incendiary bombs and pouring gasoline on civilian homes; while on the ground, they blocked the roads and shot fleeing residents.

Colossal plumes of smoke were suffocating the rattling throats of the dying, while the long, fiery tongues licked the blood-soaked living.

On September 8th, the Japanese Air Force bombarded Songjiang Station. With eight airplanes, they targeted a ten-car train carrying refugees. During the fifty-minute siege, they dropped seventeen bombs. When the airplanes

---

29. It is unclear which writer Hasegawa is referring to here.

first flew around the train, the refugees packed inside hardly suspected the catastrophe to come. All of a sudden, the bombs fell, destroying the last four cars. Flesh, blood, and tearful cries shot out in every direction. Those who were not wounded rushed out of the untouched cars. Then, a bomb hit the front of the train, killing everyone inside. Around the station, people were running in bloody bedlam. The airplanes hunted them down, flying low to the ground, shooting at them with their machine guns. The legs of man are no match for the wings of airplanes. They fell one after another. One last group ran desperately into the fields. Following them, the machine guns worked hard. The group hid itself in a massive quarry, and thanked the gods for protecting them. But the airplanes spotted them, and on that location dropped three bombs, one after another, each of which exploded in the quarry, burying in moments the mass of people within.

—Ba Jin, writing to Yamakawa Hitoshi[30]

Quiet Was the Early Autumn Day in the French Park

The high blue sky was without a single cloud. On the green grass, white and yellow chrysanthemums were putting forth their sweet fragrance. Here and there walked men with cigarettes in their mouths, or young lovers, arm in arm. Among these Chinese, one could also see a few Sikh policemen. Brown faces with thick beards, white turbans wrapped around their heads. They carried short cudgels, which seemed unnecessary here, as they walked back and forth, listlessly, robotically. One of them stopped before a monkey cage, and a large childish grin broke out across his bearded face. He called out to one of the monkeys

---

30. Ba Jin (1904–2005): An anarchist, novelist, and translator. He was also, if briefly, a prominent Esperantist. Yamakawa Hitoshi (1880–1958): A revolutionary socialist who played a leading role in founding the Japanese Communist Party in 1922.

in a gentle, friendly manner, and with his cudgel gave a few soft taps to its red bottom through the bars. The monkey didn't mind. It knew him well. Finally, he withdrew from his pocket some high-quality sweets, tore open the beautiful wrapping of one, and threw it into his mouth. Then he gave one to each of the monkeys.

Boom! A cannon roared, startling the tranquil air. The walkers stopped in their tracks and then, as if nothing had happened, resumed what they were doing. The park became quiet again, quieter even than before.

Silver airplanes appeared on the blue canvas of sky. With lightning speed, they swooped down, dropped bombs, and flew away. One of the planes exploded and disappeared from sight, leaving behind only a trail of white cloud.

The people on the sun-soaked grass watched on, with hands held above their brows, as if they were watching an air show.

I, too, a Japanese woman married to a Chinese man, was walking among the sweet-smelling white and yellow chrysanthemums. But I was not calm. A thousand words that I wanted to say to the Chinese people lay hopelessly at the bottom of my heart. Ten thousand words that I wanted to scream at the Japanese soldiers, who were likely very close by, were pushing their way through my throat. Those soldiers who were massacring the Chinese were themselves victims of the Japanese fascists. Inevitably, they too would be wounded and die. They were spilling the blood of their neighbors as well as that of their own, for the enemy. My words were trapped inside of me without an outlet, by something invisible, untouchable, yet strong, against which I had no way to protest or complain. "Is this not what you wanted?" a mocking voice sounded from within. I bit my lips and whispered to myself: "One day, things will be different...." But when would that day be?

I walked with Ren, like the other couples, among the white and yellow chrysanthemums. And quiet was the early autumn day in the French park.

Who Is to Blame?

I did not like to enter C.'s room, even though I spent my first two days in Shanghai there.

The room had once been characterized by the simple order of a bachelor salaried worker. Then everything changed. The air became suffocating, reeking of tobacco, brandy, and male body odors, among other nauseating smells. On the floor and table were strewn several empty bowls, plates, and tumblers. From morning to night, C. and his friends, all unemployed because of the war, drank, smoked, chatted, and played mahjong. I say "from morning to night," but in truth there was no clear division of time. For this small group of idle men, day was often night, and night was often day.

The reason I did not like to enter his room was not only because of the bad smells and uncleanliness. It was also hard for me to see youths like that in such times. So did I hate C.? That seems to me to be another matter entirely.

Of his background, I knew little. I knew that he was from the same province as Ren; that they had met at university; that he had taken part in the movement and, after the Manchurian Incident, had stopped going home, for home had become hell, while the invaders called it "paradise."[31] Afterward, he went to Germany to study architecture and, on returning to China, got a job as a civil engineer at Shanghai City Hall.

He was short in stature but carried himself like a European. He could dance, and sometimes took us to the dance halls. He was very skilled at dancing and stood out from other Chinese men. However, I did not find any joy or vigor in his dancing. Rather, the impression I had was that he was an automaton. His lips were always stretched in a smile, but not the smile of

---

31. The movement: Hasegawa could be referring to the Esperanto, labor, or May Fourth movement, but this individual's identity has not been confirmed.

somebody really smiling. His teeth and the tip of his right middle finger were yellow from too much smoking. He was about thirty years old but looked middle-aged, and not just because of his missing front tooth and receding hairline. Although his financial situation could have easily allowed him to marry, he never did, nor did he search for a partner. I once saw a photograph of him among a German family. Standing beside him was a pretty young woman. I heard that they had been in a romantic relationship, one that ended unhappily for him. Whether that was true or not, I never found out.

His bookcase held several Marxist works, no mere decorations. I often saw him fervently discussing various social problems with his friends.

Was he chatty or quiet? He seemed both. We only exchanged a few words, of which I remember him saying: "I don't like Shanghai. I prefer Beijing."

Day after day, week after week, month after month. Was there something, somewhere, for this lonely technocrat to do? First his clothes and bedding disappeared, then he sent away a box of books that we had been keeping in his room.

Could the invaders not foresee that the Chinese army would be so persistent in their resistance? The Chinese kept fighting yet had difficulty beating back the modern weapons of the enemy, amassed over years. At last, there came the day that had to come sooner or later. On the twenty-seventh of October, the Chinese army withdrew its forces from Shanghai. Three months was too short a time to get satisfactory results.

But the War of Resistance continued.

Indeed, China kept up its resistance after Shanghai fell into the enemy's hands, followed by Beijing and Tianjin. As if to symbolize this tenaciousness, the next day there appeared above the Sihang Warehouse by the Suzhou River the flag of the blue sky and bright sun.[32] Inside the warehouse, Chinese soldiers had barricaded themselves, not wanting to retreat. The waving flag lit up the gray hearts of the citizens, though that light was to be extinguished soon after. Thousands of people came to see it from across the river dividing the concession from the occupied area, and C. was among them.

With a friend, C. climbed onto a nearby balcony to better see the flag. He did not at all notice that behind him people were whispering.

"Here's a suspicious character! Look, he's wearing one of those black suits the European bastards love so much."

The whispers grew louder, spreading like ripples through the street. When C. at last came down, he found himself face-to-face with an angry mob. Some questions were asked, and he tried to answer them. But in the end, the mob did not sufficiently understand him, nor he it. For he was the native son of a distant northeastern province. His friend, too, had yet to master the local Shanghainese dialect.

"Traitor!"

The crowd began to shout in his face. The two men desperately tried to explain themselves, but it was no use.

"Beat the traitor!"

"Beat him to death!"

C's friend ran off to a nearby police station and came back with a policeman. But it was too late. C. lay on the ground, breathless and bloodied. There was absolutely nothing that the police could do against such a mass of people.

During his life, C. had been struck by some unexpected emotional crisis. At his death, he was struck by an unexpected physical blow. But we could not and would not avenge his death. Should he now be in the world beyond, perhaps he is looking

---

32. A reference to the then national flag of China.

down on us, a twisted smile of resignation stretched across his battered face.

"Now It Is Winter"

With the cessation of cannon fire and shelling, Shanghai became consumed by a frosty silence. How the wind cut to the bone! Was it blowing from where freshly spilled blood was now freezing over? Like stray dogs, refugees blackened either side of every street. The price of goods soared terribly high. Vegetables especially rose to double, triple what they had cost before. Meat and rice became pretty much unattainable. "We're not selling," the rice vendors said coldly, while they kept their own pantries full. One time we came upon the closed door of a rice vendor, on which was posted a sign reading "Open Today." From the early hours of morning, people had been crowding before it. Everybody was dressed in dirty and miserable tatters, with bags or baskets gripped in their hands. They pushed and shoved while women and children wept. From an elevated height, a policeman swung his cudgel above their heads. When the vendor would start selling was anyone's guess.

Broadsides and anti-Japanese posters, which not so long ago had strongly attracted passersby, had all but disappeared. Two Chinese dailies shut down operations, a fate perhaps waiting for others. It was strictly forbidden to do or say anything that would upset the Japanese authorities. Many intellectuals who had been active before the war, and would be during it—even under raining bullets—fled to Hankou or elsewhere.

The capital city of Nanjing was in danger. Now the invaders were beginning to stretch their talons even to the concessions of Shanghai. The Safety Zone was increasingly losing its meaning. How long would we have to hold out without bread and freedom here? Escape had long stood as an inevitable problem before us. But where to, and how? For us, every road seemed too narrow, and here the situation was becoming more urgent with every passing day. After discussing the matter with some friends, we finally decided to flee south. We wanted, or more precisely, we "dreamed" of going to Hankou, the new center of the resistance, by way of Hong Kong and Guangzhou. Ah, if only we could reach it! It wouldn't even matter if I was arrested the moment I disembarked. But was it not possible that something terrible could happen to us on the way? Our friends, our cohabitants during our first months in Shanghai, introduced us to Chen Yangao, a print worker, and his wife, who were willing to travel with us to Hong Kong, their native home, a city where people spoke a southern dialect that was like a foreign language for people from the other provinces.

November 26—
    Our rickshaw crawled along the streets, now brightly lit, where a few well-dressed men and women walked, now dark and miserable, where countless refugees slept like corpses covered with tattered rags. The cold evening wind cut our cheeks. Behind me sat Ren. In front of me rose the large upper body of Ye Laishi, who sat motionless. He was accompanying us to our ship and would also be going to Hankou later on. How could we, who had spent our last yuan a week prior, have made it without him? Without a word, he had done everything for us. And I never said so much as a "thank you" to him. Do people even have words to express themselves in such circumstances?
    The quay and ship swelled with people and luggage. We were ushered into a cabin, half-lit and stifling, with only one window and a small lamp. I sat down, and my head touched the bottom of a stranger's bunk.
    "There's no such thing as absolute freedom," I consoled myself. "To gain freedom, one must endure some other constraint."
    Beside me was Ren, who, because of his height, could not lie at full length. How much suffering he had to endure because of me! He often told me that he knew what he was getting into

back when we were in Tokyo. But when would his suffering and sacrifice end? Would they wither and die without bearing fruit?

I listened to the sound of the waves breaking against the hull, though not with my ears.

If only I were not such a burden...

I quickly swept away a senseless image. Forging new paths and uninterrupted construction. Was there not something else in store for our common life? Especially now, when exterior, invisible forces were so overpowering?

I felt my heart brighten. In the darkness, behind closed eyes, I conjured up our future together, though it appeared to me only vaguely....

"Now it is winter. It has only just arrived."

Traveling South

November 27—

Our ship set sail at seven o'clock in the morning, full of people and goods. The cabin we were assigned to was normally occupied by laborers. For a dozen or so yuan, we rented one of their board-like cots and a small space to put our belongings. That's right; in addition to the ticket, each passenger had to "buy a spot" for their body and bags. As a result, the crew had grown fatter with each voyage. But we should not reproach them for unjustly profiting off the national catastrophe. For had they only carried the required number of passengers, more people would have surely suffered. To be able to purchase safe passage for a small sum was a good deal, all things considered.

Our one-porthole cabin was illuminated during the day by a small electric lamp, not that I made much use of it. After all, we mostly slept, pretending that I was unwell. In Shanghai, there circulated a rumor that this ocean liner was often stopped by Japanese warships and that, sometimes, the enemy took young people from one ship or another and bayoneted them to death on the spot. In all honesty, nobody knew if this was true or not.

However, as they say, "There is no smoke without fire." Besides, I had a fear to which others could not relate. I had mentally prepared a line of answers in response to the questions "What is your name?" "Where are you going?" and so forth. But would I be asked these questions just as my friend had told me that I would?

As had been the case eight months before, the waves rocked me uneasily, lulling me to some unknown place, some nebulous future....

Our cot faced the outside, separated by a wall. Feeling the waves growing higher and higher, I sat up, hoping that this would bring me some relief, which it did not. Again I lay down and turned over, but this did not help much either. The ship would climb a mountain of waves only to plunge a moment later into a valley. But it did not merely go up and down. It also shook from side to side. And each time it did, my body rolled, my heart tightening. Every nerve in my brain was on the verge of bursting, insignificant thoughts coming and going without order. Fragments of incomprehensible Chinese spoken by my cabinmates uncomfortably brushed against my ears. I wanted nothing, absolutely nothing, but to sleep—if only it were possible to do so. Behind my closed eyes, innumerable small dots of black and blue swirled, ebbing and flowing, ebbing and flowing.

Next to us were a dozen students from Shanghai University. They told us that they were traveling to Hong Kong to continue their studies, which had been interrupted by the war. For these youths, who went from one land to another, life was one big song, feast, and joke. I could not fathom how they could stay so happy and content on such accursed bunks. To me, they seemed like men from another planet.

Things were becoming ever more unbearable for me. There was nothing to distract myself with. We had left all our books with our friends in another cabin, as it would be safer for us without such objects should we be subjected to an inspection. Even if I had a book with me, the terrible swaying, the stifling air, and the half-lit lamp would have prevented me from reading. Ren told me to not think about the waves, that I should talk more, in order to block them out. But about what? And in what language? Besides, I was not especially thinking about the waves until, all of a sudden, they would strike the side of the ship, which would then let out a disagreeable, metallic creak. Moreover, my entire body was rolling, as if everything inside of it were in a state of revolt. I turned myself to the dark and dirty wall, holding fast to the side of our cot. *I want it to go away, all of it! I don't want anything, anything at all!* My head throbbed. It hurt so much that I wanted to vomit.

Time crawled, as if it had no desire to move forward. The lamp tinted my surroundings in a sickly hue from morning to night. The same, always the same. Fatigue and apathy built a nest in me, and I had no strength to resist them. From time to time, the abrupt movement of the waves, from peak to valley, gave me a sick joy, replaced a moment later with hellish torture that never stopped to bite and chafe me.

In the middle of the night, the shaking became violent beyond words. Yet everybody in our cabin was asleep. Some were even rocking like babies. Outside, there sounded something like a whistle and a ghastly moan.

Were we heading into a storm?

November 28—

The morning sunlight forced its way through the cabin porthole. I went outside for the first time since boarding.

The sky was calm, with only a few signs of the evening's rainfall. The steel, unroofed deck was full of people and things. One could scarcely find room to walk, there was so much luggage! Chairs, tables, woks—even chamber pots... People had brought everything with them, as if some among them had feared losing a single pair of chopsticks!

The ship's crew shouted as they brought out large tubs of leftover rice, pushing themselves with difficulty through the crowd of people and their effects. Everybody ran to them at once, filling large bowls to the brim, or pots that were presumably meant for a family. Several women skillfully started fires in washbasins and, as if they were at home, cooked up vegetables, meat, or else made congee from the provided leftover rice. Not feeling very hungry, I looked away from them. To my right, behind a mountain of belongings, I saw some men sitting on the deck, gambling. Two women—their wives, most likely—watched uncomfortably nearby, their eyes focused now on one hand, now on the other, and at the same time on the paper bills set out in the middle.

The water was still. Only here and there did white froth rise and fall on the emerald surface, tracing incalculable beautiful designs. A short distance away, some islands draped in verdigris were enjoying a quiet slumber while floating mistily above them was a violet cloud in a sky that had taken on a gentle shade of blue. Seagulls flying blackly like thin paper cranes suddenly cast themselves down into the brilliant sea, snow-white breasts first, and at once returned to the brilliant sky. An eternal peace seemed to reign over the two firmaments and also the space between them.

Pushing and being pushed, squeezing and being squeezed, each group in the crowd held its ground, filling its lungs with the fresh, salty air of the morning. Airplanes, cannons, blood, corpses—where had they all gone? Even enemy warships were no longer a thing to be feared. There were no radios, no newspapers. Here the wind did not cut you to the bone but was soft and almost springlike in its embrace.

Charged with the fears and hopes of three hundred refugees, the ship pushed south, plying the water black and white on either side.

Noon followed morning but brought only more of the same. Every hour doubled, tripled, quadrupled in length. So allow me to skip over this long and uneventful day, for it was not until evening that something new was seen by these eyes worn down by the half light of my cabin and the monotonous blue of sea and sky.

★

The crimson sun crept ever so slowly to the horizon, on which lay a gray cloudmass. The east was already covered in a cool veil of black and blue.

The sun was beginning to hide behind the clouds. Minute by minute...inch by inch. It was not hard to make out the pink semicircle through the thin gray clouds. One minute, another...and it was gone. In the air, countless dots of red and blue trembled before eyes that until then had been fixed on the sunset.

Thick plumes of fuzzy black smoke from the smokestack crawled away like a horde of demons. From on high, seagulls shot down like arrows into the black water beneath the smoke, then swooped back up, tracing curves in the air. This they did several times, to catch fish. A cold wind blew above the dark sea.

The students were listening to records of Chinese opera, the metallic singing of which pierced my ears. The dark, cellar-like room was so thick with smoke that it made me ill, and the waves, which had just started to pick up, shook my entire body. The pain in my head was unbearable, as if every fiber of my brain had become tangled up in a big mass. I lay on my bunk, my face to the black, dusty wall, and shutting my eyes tight, covered my head with a blanket. A succession of strange sounds, first soft, then loud, creaked and cracked, together with words that were utterly incomprehensible to me. Everyone, including Ren, was listening with glee, now praising this, now criticizing that. I felt alone, left out. The metallic voice of the opera singer, which seemed to issue not from the larynx but from the forehead, shredded me to pieces. All the while, the malicious waves outside rose ever higher and higher. My heart ached. I started to weep uncontrollably. Ren seemed so distant to me now. I felt like a spoiled little girl who, in the midst of a fever, nervously complains about the distance between her and her lover....Ren reproached my bourgeois softness, scolded me for isolating myself, and told me that I was being unfaithful to him.

I went up to the deck alone. The people who had been there earlier were now asleep. There were no signs of the morning's chaos. Out on the vast sea there twinkled not even one small light. No moon, no stars. Just darkness, total, all-consuming darkness. Only the waves gnashed their white teeth in a disquieting swell of water. A cold chill ran through my heart, followed by a light laugh in my belly—I knew not why. I stealthily crept back downstairs, where I was confronted by the angry but at the same time concerned face of Ren.

November 29—

From early morning, everybody was waiting for our arrival at the port of Shantou as if they were to be set free from prison. The students carefully washed their faces, greased their hair, and brushed off their clothes and shoes.

Shantou is a small but pretty city that intersects with the Tropic of Cancer. Behind the harbor rise low hills. On both sides of the well-swept streets are lined tropical trees with dense, green foliage. Next to them stand shops selling reams of snow-white lace and brightly colored embroidery, the famous products of the city.

Red-lacquered rickshaws with spotless cushions quietly ran along the noiseless morning streets. After a half-hour walk, we arrived at Zhongshan Park, on the edge of the city. In the park and along the streets were what appeared to be air-raid shelters. But nowhere was there to be seen a sign of wartime tension.

All along the harbor, half-naked men in the happy sunlight were contentedly eating their lunches. The harbor was overflowing with merchants selling all kinds of fruits—oranges, bananas, lemons—and buns. In several places, making use of the small space available to them, people had set up food stalls. Meats, vegetables, noodles, live and skipping prawns...An old man with healthy sun-kissed skin skillfully cooked them up in several minutes. How attractive for the wearied travelers was the green of the vegetables and the red of the prawns! They came one after another, holding small coins or paper money, and left comfortably satiated. Each time the mass of raw materials diminished, a full-cheeked boy—likely the grandson of the old man—ran out to bring back more ingredients. A group of Shanghainese laborers, delighted by the inexpensive cost of everything, bought without let, as if they had suddenly become millionaires, eating as if their stomachs had become bottomless. Here, one's money had three to five times the value that it had in Shanghai. This was especially true if you were buying oranges—oh, those sweet and succulent Shantou oranges! Back in the spring, when I had been laid down by a bad cold, I had felt a strong desire for fruit, which was a total luxury for us. Nevertheless, Ren had bought me some oranges at a cost of fifteen cents each, which, while no steal, was cheaper than buying apples. Here oranges cost one cent! So we bought a lot and were beyond content with the taste. From our basket, they smiled at me like gold, filling me with bright, childlike joy.

From ship to port, from port to ship, there flowed a steady stream of men, loading and unloading goods. Brown, strong-bodied southern men, scarcely clad in worn-out gray clothes—which here did not look sad because of the mild, tropical weather—came and went with heavy packages. Their unintelligible cries were like the roars of wild animals.

In the evening, at five o'clock, the ship pulled up anchor. On the shore, a dozen men and women, aged six to sixty, were collecting half-empty bags of flour that had been left behind. There was enough for each to feed a family.

The murky water of the harbor, on which floated oil, fruit rinds, cigarette butts, and pieces of paper, receded farther and farther into the distance. Twilight descended on the sea. Lights in the hills blinked faintly. The wind was cold.

All of a sudden, I stood nailed to my spot. There, on the same deck, only a couple of meters away, stood a Japanese couple! They were definitely Japanese, though the man wore a European suit and the woman a modern Chinese qipao. Perhaps they had noticed me too, for they quickly and stealthily went below deck.

Later we were told by Chen the print worker that they were the Kajis.

Kaji Wataru![33]

The name was not at all foreign to me. I knew him as an old member of the defunct Japanese Union of Proletarian Writers. Before I left Japan, a magazine editor had suggested that I visit Kaji and ask him to help me with my translations and writing. I never took up his suggestion in the end, considering all the trouble it might cause both him and me. But here he was, in the flesh. Well! A chance meeting of three same-fated Japanese people! A brief and mute one at that. It was said that they were preparing to return home but had been unable to secure a ship and were now fleeing to Hong Kong to avoid the persecution of the Japanese fascists. We did not see them again, even at our disembarking in Hong Kong. Surely they had felt uneasy about my appearance, an unknown Japanese woman whom they could not easily judge to be a friend or foe.

Besides, I had no words of consolation to say to them.

P.S. Shantou remains in my mind a peaceful, friendly, and quiet city, though it has now long been occupied by the Japanese Army and is a shadow of its former self. I will not write of the ruin it faced after burning, pillaging, and massacres. However, I do have one piece of heartrending news—and one is too much!—which is that in Shantou I am told they no longer sell rice by the liter, nor by the kilogram, but by the *gram!*

December 1—

It was in the morning that our ship reached Hong Kong. Even in the harbor, the sea had a marvelous emerald

---

33. Kaji Wataru (1901–1982): The pseudonym of Seguchi Mitsugi, a novelist. Charged with violating Japan's Peace Preservation Law, he fled to China in 1936, where he married the dissident Ikeda Yuki. He later worked with Hasegawa in the Japanese People's Anti-War Alliance.

sheen. A little farther off, the surface of the water was smooth and specked with steamships bearing British flags and black schooners. Nothing moved, as if glued to the spot.

On the harbor front stood a row of large hotels, pressed closely together. Behind them rose large green hills, from which pompous cream-colored mansions arrogantly looked down. On the paved main thoroughfare, Westerners in light clothing were walking briskly, and Chinese dandies strolled unencumbered, arm in arm.

Meanwhile, the misery of China thronged on the quay. Sly rickshaw drivers, stevedores with ropes and poles, and newsies of every age shouted argumentatively at the disembarking passengers. Barefoot women in black blouses and trousers, under wide-brimmed tasseled hats that protected their faces against the sun, deftly loaded boats with goods lowered from the steamships anchored a short distance away. With crude oars in their strong, callused hands, they rowed to shore.

December 2—

The newspapers informed us that the Japanese army was parading through the international concessions of Shanghai.

Meanwhile, how different things were in Hong Kong— this beautiful island, independent from the mainland. Even the people here lived independently. For a few dollars, the customs officers let us have our typewriter, about which we had been anxious. They stood on their feet all day long, neither for the British Empire, nor for the Republic of China.

Oh, if only we could be in Guangzhou already! There, the Esperanto movement was going strong, and Ren would be able to find work through friends if we could not go straight to Hankou. But we had to wait until we had good escorts. The print worker Chen and his wife would not be coming with us, for they had not been able to procure the money needed to go to Hankou. Besides, they were from Hong Kong and knew people here. They could make it, while we could not....

December 3—

It was seven thirty in the morning. Our ship was about to leave for Guangzhou, but our escorts had yet to arrive. We were anxious, on edge. Standing next to us was Little Chen, a Hong Kong Esperantist who had seen me off in Yokohama eight months prior. Everybody called him the Ethiopian because of the darkness of his skin and because his innocent, good nature was like that of an African native. When Ren asked him to go look for our escorts, he wordlessly ran into the mass of people like a child sent on an errand. A few minutes later, he came back looking ashamed, as if he had done something wrong.

"They're not here yet," he said timidly. "I wonder what could be keeping them?"

Then Ren went off in a huff but came back in vain as well.

The gong signaling our departure sounded. Merchants and well-wishers began to disembark. Our six eyes impatiently and nervously watched the harbor. But our escorts did not appear. The gangplank was being readied for removal. Like a scared hare, Little Chen leapt from the ship in a few bounds, without so much as a word of farewell.

"..."

"No matter. We'll go alone. Everything will be all right." Ren tried to force a smile.

As the ship picked up speed, Ren spread out a newspaper he had bought. It was the previous day's paper, not that he noticed. Around us, people were chirping, clucking, and croaking while we sat mute, estranged, and alone.

In Guangzhou

My First Step on Truly Chinese Soil

Hardly had we sat down in our rickshaw to go to our hotel when out of the mass of people in the port came a short man with a disagreeable face who ordered our driver to halt. Heavens! My heart stopped. Did I not foresee such a thing happening to us? But why now, when we were on our own?

I felt the earth open up beneath me.

The man spoke to Ren, first in Cantonese, then in English. A crowd started to gather, but the man shooed them away in a severe tone.

"Is she your wife?"

"Yes."

"I've been told she's Japanese."

"No, she's not. But her parents were immigrants, so she doesn't speak Chinese well."

The man eyed me with suspicion but asked no questions. Then came the Ws, the escorts we had been waiting for in Hong Kong. Ah, so they had all been on board all along! How the devil had we missed them?

A few minutes later, we were sitting in a comfortable room of the first-class New Asia Hotel. High ceilings, a large clean bed, a porcelain floor decorated with geometric tiles. With our featherlight wallet, we should have been staying in a small rural inn. But this time it was absolutely necessary that we make ourselves appear rich.

The detective, the Ws, and Ren entered into another round of interrogation in English. I listened to them impatiently, watching, with unease, these people who were ultimately to decide my fate. The subject of their discussion was, of course, myself. But the detective never turned to me with questions. He still suspected that I was Japanese but had no way to prove it. The others protested that I was Chinese, but they, too, were unable to give proof. Mrs. W, who had edited a women's magazine in Shanghai, and her husband were newcomers in our life. When we arrived in Hong Kong, they had been introduced to Ren as people who were willing to help us. And now they were defending me, a helpless, Japanese woman, as if we had long been friends.

The position in which Ren had been placed could not have

been easy, for while the truth flowed straight from his mouth, the lies came out in zigzags. He kept stammering and pausing. This could have aroused more suspicion in the detective. Fortunately, however, they were all speaking English, so fluency was not expected in the first place. Moreover, Ren kept throwing in Esperanto words unconsciously. He said *ne* instead of "no," *kompreneble* instead of "of course," *milito* instead of "war." Recognizing this, he corrected himself over and over again, not that this helped our case at all.

The detective went away and returned with his superior and a colleague, at which point there ensued a third round of interrogation. I knew well that we were in the middle of a war and that these men were only faithfully carrying out their duty to the nation. However, how could I love and respect them while they were ganging up to attack my poor husband with such severity! After half an hour, thanks to the help of the Ws, and with explanations from Ren, especially concerning his work in Shanghai, the three men stood up and gave a civil salute of farewell. But before they left, they warned Ren that if I were, in fact, Japanese, he would have to leave me in accordance with the wartime directive and that I should not go outside lest some mob beat me by accident.

It was unclear whether the men were convinced that I was Chinese or, knowing the truth and finding me harmless, had decided to let me go. In either case, we could breathe easy. That which we had feared most had not come to pass.

"I'm the one who's guilty, yet you're the one who took the lashing...."

"Don't be silly. I would do anything for you. Besides, everything went well."

Ren's hair was disheveled from our ocean voyage. He looked exhausted. But instead of sitting down, he just paced back and forth restlessly.

After dinner and a bath, I stood at the window, looking

down on the illuminated streets. Pale emptiness and black dread alternated within me.

What would tomorrow bring? Without money or guarantees... Oh well, tomorrow was tomorrow, and today we were still alive. Only the clean, soft bed could hold our attention after our harrowing week-long voyage at sea.

To sleep, then! Deep sleep!
Que será, será!

In a Desert

We had hoped to go straightaway to Hankou, to publicly take part in the War of Resistance. It was the heart of Fighting China, where people would surely understand our situation. We would throw ourselves into anti-invasion and Esperanto work. But how far away it was from here! It was a four-day journey by train. That itself was not so long, but we would have to factor in several days of refuge during enemy air strikes and the repair of bombed-out rail tracks. This, too, was no big deal, for until now we had never heard of such a thing happening. The real problem was that we would require sufficient escorts to protect me. Every day, people were going to Hankou by the hundreds. But who would have the goodwill to take a Japanese woman with them? Another problem was money. The cost of the voyage aside, in a few days we wouldn't have any money for bread. The money we had borrowed from Ye Laishi had nearly been spent. He and several of our closest comrades were still in Shanghai. Sooner or later, they would go to Hankou to continue the Esperanto movement. But nobody knew when. Only the military situation could decide.

If we were wanderers in a desert, Esperantists were our oasis. On our second day in Guangzhou, we visited Comrade Chen Yuan, a pen pal of Ye and the editor of *Al nova etapo*. On the third day, Chen and his comrades, all of whom were students at Sun Yat-sen University, brought us to a cheaper hotel, for we no longer needed to pretend to be wealthy. They told us that Comrade T.

was staying here. Comrade T. had taken part in the fiftieth anniversary celebration of Esperanto as the representative from Guangzhou. I had gone out with her a few times back in Shanghai, and she had made a good impression on me. Surely we could ask her for help. Unfortunately, on the day that we arrived she had left for Hong Kong and would not be back for a whole week.

If only the Cantonese friends I had made in Tokyo were here! Especially Deng Keqiang—but he was still in jail. When would we see him again?

Then, totally unexpectedly, one of those comrades came to us accompanied by Comrade Chen. This was Comrade D. On seeing him, Ren's face lit up. Because we could not go to Hankou, Ren had to look for work here, and the most pressing thing was to secure lodging and enough money to get by on. Ren told Comrade D. everything, believing that he could, and would, do all in his power to help us.

Comrade D. saw us a few times a day, and each time the hope on Ren's face waned a little bit more.

"Why not?" Ren grumbled spitefully. "Is he not capable of accomplishing such a small task? In Tokyo, he lived a life of luxury. His family was rich, and his father had lots of influence. Moreover, he is now an official!"

Eventually, one night when we were walking on a half-lit street, Ren confessed to me: "You know, having rich friends means nothing."

I could only respond with bitter silence.

We continued to refer to D. as our comrade, but what kind of camaraderie tied him to us? Here, he took part in neither the Esperanto nor the national liberation movements. He had become a typical government official. And what could we ask from a typical government official?

"Let him choose his own path!"

I kicked a stone with the tip of my shoe.

★

Ren suffered from an eczema-related foot pain, which the people in Guangzhou referred to as "Hong Kong foot disease."[34] Still, he kept going out to look for work. Where and whom to, I never found out. Aside from the Esperantists, he probably met up with the "Shanghai intellectuals" with whom he was somewhat acquainted. I don't know by whose grace we were able to eat two times a day.

"Don't lose heart," Ren would say to me. "Stay positive, and I will do everything I can for us." So like a spoiled, helpless child, I sat around with nothing to do while he alone planned, begged, and suffered.

One time only did he ever express that he might be in over his head. At the time, he was not thinking about his home in the northeast nor I about my home in Tokyo, which we had willingly forsaken for a free and meaningful life....

We waited impatiently for the return of Comrade T. This young student from Sun Yat-sen University was our only hope.

Finally, she appeared before us, paid for our hotel stay, and took me to where she and her friends were working to save China. At first Ren decided that it would be best if he stayed with some old friends from Beijing he had run into. But two days later, he came to us, for some of these friends had abruptly left for Hankou, and the others, from a lack of money, were set to move into a cheap and shabby lodging house.

A Band of Youths

It stood in a low-income neighborhood of the city. Formerly a private middle school, it had long since closed down for some reason. In addition to a small gymnasium with a basketball court, the two-story building, with its damp kitchen and rural bathroom full of filth and maggots, consisted of several rooms, in one of which lay a disorganized mess of dusty books, wastepaper, and other bits of detritus. To be sure, from the outside it may have

---

34. A reference to athlete's foot.

looked like a ruin, but from the inside there glowed another kind of life. A dozen youths, students of Sun Yat-sen University, lived there and, along with other comrades, worked for the so-called national salvation movement.

Day and night, they held regular meetings or conducted courses—instruction in Cantonese Latinxua and patriotic songs for children belonging to the families of poor merchants and laborers and classes on linguistics and phonetics. Besides this, they discussed social issues, attended party meetings, took classes at the university, wrote articles, printed materials, and made broadsides and comics for the bourgeoisie.

Although I hardly understood the content of their work, I could tell that they were all inexperienced, doing everything formulaically and on an all-too-limited scale. That said, their youthful enthusiasm made up for just about everything, revivifying the half ruin in which they operated, giving it life and light. Aside from basketball, their sole form of amusement was singing. They often belted patriotic songs and hummed unconsciously during work. The songs were an inseparable extension of themselves.

As all of the students were young, their days shone bright, as did their tireless work.

Comrades T., Wo Dan, and R. lived in the room next to ours. Comrade T., who had brought us here and who took great care of us, was the only woman in the group. Her family lived by the Zhujiang River, and she had to visit them from time to time. She said that her parents had conservative beliefs and did not want her hanging around with so many men. Simply clothed, intellectual, eloquent, and kind—she was the very model of a modern Chinese woman. The hardest worker of the bunch, she slept only five hours each night and often ate only one meal a day due to a lack of time.

Comrade Wo was an orphan from Taiwan, who had lived on the mainland since childhood. He was tall, lean, and athletic. He did not talk much but liked to eat and in spite of his age maintained a childlike naivety. When he laughed, he exposed his pure white teeth, and his eyes became thin behind his thick glasses.

These two youths were clearly in love. But they did not have time for sweet nothings. Besides, they seemed to derive an inexhaustible joy from their common labor and gay singing, taking delight in a life that was in harmony with their enthusiasm for work and love of comradery. On their seldom free nights, they sang popular songs like "Home! Sweet Home!," "My Old Kentucky Home," and "Serenade." One could not but feel one's heart melt on hearing the soprano and bass ranges of their voices pleasingly ring out through the warm air of the tropical December evening.

Comrade R. was a sickly boy. His face was round, pale, and bore a gentle smile. However, he was not at all happy when I first met him. He was in love with a Taiwanese girl who had worked as a nurse in Shanghai. Two months before we had arrived in Guangzhou, she had been arrested and sent to a jail outside the city.

"As you know, a large number of Taiwanese people work as spies for the Japanese imperialists. So they arrested her! We will only be able to free her after the war. But who knows what will happen in the meantime...."

Comrade R. lowered his gaze sadly, and there passed a moment of silence between us.

Then, putting his hand on mine, he said, sighing: "She is short and stout like you. Oh how happy you must be to have your husband with you."

Our room was the only room that had previously been unoccupied, as it had functioned as both a pantry and a sort of wastepaper basket. Out of two benches and a few tables, we made ourselves a makeshift bed.

The students were kind to us. They let us freely read their newspapers and books. Besides, the cost of living was low. The two of us could eat well in working-class cafeterias every day for a Guangdong half yuan, one yuan of which was equivalent to eighty fen of the national currency. Under such circumstances, we could manage to get by if we borrowed a little from friends, or sold or pawned our clothing.

When one of Ren's friends who had lacked money to go

to Hankou told us he was planning on hitching a ride on a military train or traveling cheaply with a discounted group ticket, we proposed joining him. However, things did not go how he or we wanted. Whether we liked it or not, we would have to stay here, where Ren had no hope of finding work. Because of the linguistic barrier, he could not even take part in the national salvation movement. Although we were still young, we had to wait and wait, while all around us, other young people were working so hard.

In the evenings, while the electrically lit classroom was occupied by a class or meeting, we would walk in the streets, where we felt even more alone. Guangzhou is not Shanghai, where one may encounter all kinds of people, from everywhere in and beyond China. Many curious eyes clung to me. Several passersby even turned around to look at me. Did they suspect that I was Japanese, or simply a stranger?

Listlessly would we return to our dark room, light a candle, and try to read or write, but there was too much noise in the neighboring rooms. Moreover, when you live isolated from the outside world, everything loses its meaning and becomes tiring. We wanted to do something useful for others. But what could we do?

> I wish to find
> a task at which I can work happily—
> Then I would accomplish it and die.

I repeated softly to myself this poem by Takuboku, which now seemed to me to be more relevant than ever before.[35]

As for Ren, he was of the opinion that we would have to get ourselves out of this situation soon. But everything was more of a dream than a plan. We were getting nervous, and the invisible tomorrow was only making us more so.

---

35. Ishikawa Takuboku (1886–1912): A poet whose later work was largely influenced by socialist thought. The poem is from his 1910 tanka collection *Ichiaku no suna*.

82 Inside Fighting China

"A Tragedy?"

Three men were sitting down together.

One of them was Guo Moruo, the famous revolutionary poet. He had lived in Japan as an exile, until the roar of the holy resistance pulled him out of hiding and away from his oracle bones. One night, he secretly boarded a fishing boat and returned to the breast of his homeland, from which he had been parted for ten years. A week later, he arrived in Guangzhou. His loved ones stayed in Japan without him: several children and a Japanese wife.

> When I left, my family wept
> Now I arrive to all of China mourning![36]

Another was Mr. U., an official who occupied a significant post in the Guangdong Army. He also had a Japanese wife, one who had borne him three children. Recently, the newspapers had written of their divorce. Did he no longer love her? No, he loved her the same as, or more than, he had before. But he had to leave her as a formality, because he was an official, because China and Japan were at war. Their elderly parents were looking after the children in his native village some distance from the city.

The third man was Ren.

Three men who were married to Japanese women were sitting down together.

Ren was an admirer of Guo's poetry. He had not visited him in Tokyo out of shame that he was a student from Manchukuo, the Japanese puppet state. Now he had come to ask him to help us get to Hankou—because Guo was not only a poet but a political leader who had served in the famous Northern Campaign and, as a result, had formed connections with the day's most important persons in government. Ren hoped and believed that

---

36. Hasegawa is quoting from a 1937 poem by Guo Moruo titled "Gui guo za yin" (Random thoughts on returning home).

the great man would understand, sympathize, and help us in whatever way he could. So he began to explain our situation, and Mr. Guo listened silently, as did Mr. U.

Ren paused, ready to make his request. Then he heard Mr. Guo mutter something that sounded like a thought that had accidentally escaped his lips.

"A tragedy."

Just that, nothing more.

The entire room fell silent like a tomb. And without speaking or moving, the three men with Japanese wives continued to sit where they were.

At last Ren stood up and said goodbye, his request falling down to the bottom of his anxious heart. Was there anything left for him to say?

We were again without hope. On the way home, Ren chewed on what Mr. Guo had said.

"A tragedy? Not at all! Our marriage is no tragedy!"

The End of the Year

On December 13, the Chinese army evacuated Nanjing. However, that defeat—in the view of Chiang Kai-shek, the generalissimo at the front—would bear no influence on the decided policy of the government to resist the Japanese invasion to the end. On the sixteenth, an address was published for the entire population, which read: "No matter what, we will never surrender. We must continue to march ever forward."

Already on November 2, the government had moved the capital to Chongqing, though the heart of Fighting China was still in Hankou. And this warmly beating heart was drawing more and more people after the fall of Nanjing. To go there from Shanghai, or from nearby cities, was now only possible by way of Guangzhou. As a result, the city had become increasingly populous and lively, not only because of the people passing through it but also because some of these newcomers intended to stay in this center of South China and resume their everyday affairs.

The year 1937 was on its way out. The streets, however, were not decorated for the New Year. The Chinese typically celebrate the New Year according to the lunar calendar. Meanwhile, in our ruinous room, we lived among piles of dust-covered papers that had never seen the sunlight. I did not leap with joy and hope, counting the days until the New Year on my fingers as I had once done as a child.

"Only ten days left...now only a week..."

There was a knock at our door.

"Oh? Has the New Year come early?"

It was Comrade Ye, thanks to whom we were able to come this far; Feng, who had rescued us from a sea of refugees; Xiao Cong, the editor of the Chinese-Esperanto dictionary; and his sister. Only one month prior, we had said goodbye to them in Shanghai, but it seemed as if an entire year had passed over since then.

Feng was the first to leave Guangzhou.

Before the invasion, he had been a romantic poet, but the Muses had flown away from him, along with his youth. He, too, had taken part in the Northern Campaign, something I had some trouble believing considering how thin he was and how bad his ears and legs were. How monotonous and gray had been his life in Shanghai, despite the fact that he had an active and well-dressed wife! His sole consolation at the time was Esperanto. In any event, he came here alone, without his wife, who, he explained, had sold her rings and furniture to pay for his travel expenses. Tears, which in ordinary days were totally foreign to her, had poured down her cheeks. Now he has flown from this fertile southern city, not to Hankou, but much closer to the infertile region that draws many youths. Close to forty years old, it is his intention to do something more impactful and significant. He no longer wishes to live the petite-bourgeois life of an urban intellectual.

"Come what may, I must go."

He was a middle-aged, thin, half-deaf, half-lame man of few words.

Xiao Cong and his sister stayed in Guangzhou, together,

in the office of the Shanghai Newspaper Company. As for Comrade Ye, he soon left for Hankou, where he was planning to work for our movement. So after a short-lived joy, we were again alone in our desert of a room. Our comrades agreed that we should not risk going to Hankou without a guarantee. Ye promised to work on our behalf, asking us to be patient a little longer. At least now the question of our living expenses was solved. The Shanghai Newspaper Company, which had recently relocated here from Shanghai, commissioned Ren to edit bimonthly English pieces for people studying the language.

Our typewriter, which had lain dormant for some time, began to make noise again. I had bought it in Tokyo for my Esperanto writing, and it had never been used for anything else. Therefore, it was more important to me than bread. However, its owner lived in the human world and could not survive on air alone.

Even if she was an Esperantist.

One Morning of the New Year

It was one of the first days of January.

The weather had turned sometime in the middle of the night. The sun was hiding behind a thick, leaden cloud. A keen, cutting wind was blowing. Dry leaves rustled as they rolled across the asphalt road. There were few people to be seen.

All of a sudden, the morning air began to shake:

Muzzles forward, march in step!
Don't wound commoners, don't shoot your own.[37]

The mighty song was accompanied by confident marching: *One, two, one, two...*

Soon there appeared an armed battalion. Cantonese soldiers, short but strong; brave and nimble. They were singing, not

---

37. From "Song of the National Salvation Army," a patriotic anti-Japanese song from 1935 with lyrics by Sai Kei.

only with their mouths, but with their entire bodies. In fact, they were not just singing; they were making their song a reality. In a short time, they would be at the front, where they would kill the enemies of China with guns that have been turned over the past few years, against their will, to face their own brothers.

Soon I could no longer see their faces, no longer hear their voices, and the city was once again steeped in an alienating chill. Men and women walked with quick, tense steps, like the people of some northern clime. Every man had his coat firmly buttoned-up. And every woman wore a long, knee-length wool shawl of gaudy red, green, or yellow, which she had likely not taken out of her wardrobe in several years. Over the road hung large banners tied to telephone poles on either side. The wind made them swell, and on each of them were printed big black characters reading: "Unite the army and the people! By our combined strength, let us defend our great Guangdong!"

A noise from afar was getting closer. It was a demonstration: students, officials, nurses, and merchants with banners showing what each group belonged to. Above their heads waved multicolored flags with various slogans.

Barefoot rickshaw drivers walked in a disorganized fashion. Their legs had lost their usual rapidity. Perhaps they were too used to running, pulling rickshaw and passenger. Their faces were a mixture of shame and severity.

Then there came a line of refugees from Shanghai. Middle-aged women and old ladies with infants on their back, young children at their sides. One child pulled the hand of a white-haired woman nearly running on her bound feet so as not to be left behind. All of the women wore rags, their faces wrinkled, their hair unkempt. Two or three boys were singing patriotic songs, or trying to. Smiles flashed across the black and pallid faces of unhappy mothers and grandmothers as the high voices of the children rang out.

Following this was a group of uniformed men from the

military training camp. Unlike their predecessors, they marched in an orderly manner: *one, two, one, two.*

Everyone was scattering colored flyers. Several youths quickly scrawled on the road in large white characters: "Let the city rise up and take arms! Kill the invaders and traitors to our country!" A four-year-old boy stepped out from the crowd and gave a joyful leap over the newly written slogan. Then an old man in rags appeared, looked around timidly, and began to collect the flyers and paper flags on the ground.

Mobilized from every part of the city, lines of ashen people marched and marched as if without end, now warming, now cooling the frosty air.

"And yet," whispered my friend, pointing to the seven-story Aiqun Hotel across the street, "do you know that such places are home to the public and semipublic traitors, who are even now getting up to no good?"

Another Side of the City

Enemy airplanes came often, but the people did not run. Even if they wanted to, they had no place to go. Sure, there were underground shelters, but those were not meant for them. After the air-raid sirens started to blare, the city would fall silent, yet several rickshaws and cars continued quietly on their way, and the police let them go without a word. When, in the evening, people extinguished their lamps to chat in the moonlight, it was as if they were simply out on a regular social call. Doubtless they were well aware that the enemy did not spare unarmed citizens. Surely they had seen many victims from Shanghai with their own eyes. Yet in spite of this, they continued to believe that the Japanese warplanes only ever aimed at military bases. And indeed, to date the Japanese had never shelled the city itself, and most often flew farther out to the airdrome beyond its limits. So it had been, and so it would continue to be. In the heads of the residents there rested this simple assumption, or hope, which they took to be an immutable fact.

The Cantonese love to *yum cha,* "to go to a tea house." Not war nor enemy planes droning overhead have power over this custom.

It is no exaggeration to say that on every street in Guangzhou stands one or more tea houses. In Xiguan, the commercial center, there are old Cantonese tea houses; on Sun Yat-sen Street, the cultural center, new European-style tea houses; and the working-class district has its own half-lit, small, or midsized ones.

If you are an educated urbanite, you would naturally like to visit the newfangled type, what with its printed menus from which you can order pretty cakes, pastries, and other dainties from young waiters with snow-white aprons. But if you are at all curious to take in the local atmosphere and traditional cuisine, you should go to Xiguan. There, from the crack of dawn, you will find many people quietly sitting in tea houses, mostly in Chinese dress, though there are few female customers to speak of.

Upon taking a seat at a Xiguan teahouse, you will be waited on by a middle-aged waiter with a dirty Chinese apron carrying a large, flat receptacle containing steamed dumplings. If dumplings are not to your liking, let him go on among the tables to the other customers. Soon similar waiters with similar-looking receptacles will come before you, one after the other, with buns, pies, ham rolls, puddings, and more. To take one plate of every dish—each plate being one to three portions—you would need a devil of a stomach.

Alternatively, if you are not afraid of the sweaty odor of workers' bodies and defective, unwashed utensils, you should at least once show up at a working-class tea house. There the taste of the dishes is something else, something quite special, really, and totally unlike what I described above. It is much cheaper, besides.

On average these dishes will cost you five cents per plate, so one yuan will go far to keep you satisfied. But true Cantonese people don't really do things this way. They will sit, slowly drink their tea, chat, smoke, and repose all morning long, yet the number of plates before them will not exceed two or three. Here, people discuss everything. Business deals, marriages, and other important matters can be solved during *yum cha*. Even if one has a small salary and a penny-pinching wife, he can still squeeze from her twenty cents and pass a good half Sunday in a tea house.

For the Cantonese, *yum cha* is a necessary part of life. It may also be thought of as a sort of consequence of circumstance. For you see, Guangzhou is located south of the Tropic of Cancer and is compassed by a vast and fertile plain, over which flow several rivers while before it stretches the sea. In such a well-situated place, people naturally have it easy. Mind you, *yum cha* in no way represents the Cantonese spirit, if such a thing exists. One hundred years ago, Guangzhou was but a lonely port at which the Chinese government uniquely permitted foreign trade to take place. Accordingly, the people there quickly picked up Western civilization and, at the same time, made progress in their ideas and actions. The majority of Chinese immigrants to Malaya, Vietnam, Burma, and the islands of the South Sea are Cantonese. With superhuman effort and persistence, they overcame innumerable difficulties in those foreign locales, sending home, year after year, large sums of money and contributing in no small way to their nation's store of wealth.

This spirit is reflected in the revolutionary history of China. The Opium Wars of the 1840s took place here, the first acts of Chinese anti-imperialism, though they were unsuccessful and left the country in an unfortunate state. During the last few decades, Guangzhou has occupied an important position in several revolutions that have aimed to destroy the feudal warring powers. Many famous revolutionaries have come from among the Cantonese people, which is why people often glorify Guangzhou as "the mainspring of the Revolution."

Since coming to China, I have often heard that Cantonese women are brave and capable, and this seems to me to be no exaggeration. But such a character did not emerge by chance, nor miracle. Furthermore, in the city there exists a special group of women composed of unschooled women who do not want to get married because they know that marriage will give them nothing but suffering and divorcees who can no longer endure abuse from their husbands and in-laws. They call each other sisters and help each other. Generally, they work as servants, and as such, they do not have true freedom. However, is it not both meaningful and interesting that these uneducated women courageously trample on traditional law, organizing themselves against the unjust treatment of women by society? Indeed, only in Guangzhou could such a thing exist.

The city of tea and revolution, Guangzhou is traversed by the Pearl River, with all of its dirty tributaries. One such water course isolates the general urban districts from Shamian, where the foreigners live out their easy lives despising tea and revolution. Indeed, water is an important means of communication for Guangzhou. On the rivers float many ships rowed by shabby-looking men and women who never come to land to do work, for the people forbid them to. They are called *danmin,* and legend has it they are the conquered indigenous people of the area.[38] Their ships are their homes and the water, their world. They are born on the water and will die on the water. Meanwhile, the men on the land hate them, and they hate them right back.

The Easy Road of Life

"Our Hero of the Resistance Has Returned!"

One morning we were surprised by an extraordinary headline on the second page of the *Jiu wang qing bao* (National Salvation Newspaper). And right next to it we saw the name "Deng Keqiang." Had our dear Comrade Deng really returned? Our hearts beating fast, we impatiently read further. "The Japanese police having finally yielded to his persistence, have decided to free him and send him home.... Yesterday our anti-Japanese hero arrived safely."

---

38. *Danmin:* An old term for a subgroup of "boat people" in China.

There was no doubt that Deng, who had helped me travel to Shanghai and whose fate I had been so anxious about, had returned. What an unexpected joy! However, one fear still obsessed me, though it was clearly printed that he had returned "safely." Was he still healthy in body and mind? In Shanghai, Huang Yihuan, who had been arrested around the same time, and under the same pretext, but who had been released earlier, had told us that the torture that Deng had to endure was so terrible that it had somewhat messed with his head. That was before the war. So it was not difficult to suppose that, afterward, he had suffered more. Moreover, he had been sitting in a prison for eight months. We knew well how the Japanese police hated and disrespected Chinese people, and the war in no way could have mollified their sentiments. If anything, it had surely made them more cruel. I imagined Deng to be pale and thin, then raving with bloodshot eyes.

Fortunately, this terrible image did not stay with me long. In fact, it disappeared like dew before the morning sun when a day later Deng showed up at our door, looking healthy, vigorous, calm, and chic as he had before. Without saying a word, we each exchanged a warm, firm, and long handshake. He had not visibly changed much between the spring and now. During the course of our conversation, I began to fear that I would find something abnormal about him. But there was nothing, absolutely nothing wrong. I wanted to cry again, with full and carefree delight: "Our hero has returned!" Or rather, I should say, "Our friend, our comrade, has returned!"

After his eight-month-long ordeal, how free the air of his native land must have seemed to him! His deceased father had been a famous revolutionary, as had his mother. Now she, already sixty years old, was the principal of a girls' school. She had a large home located outside the city. But Deng did not wish to stay there, for he was a typical youth in all senses of the word. He had to live in the city and have a more or less important position. That would be easy enough, for he had eminent relatives and acquaintances. On his third or fourth visit, he wore a handsome uniform, though soon traded it for a new European suit. With the Urban Self-Defense Union, he acquired the position of chairman, or something like that—I'm not sure what exactly. He also had to have beautiful women and eat delicious food. Indeed, everything here was very easy for him.

"Had you been a different comrade, I would not have been so anxious about your jail sentence," I jokingly confessed to him.

"Ha! You cannot imagine how well I got along with my fellow Japanese inmates, those thieves, deceivers, murderers, Reds, and whatnot!" A sincere smile ran across his lips at the recollection of friendships forged in a special world. For a moment, it was as if he had forgotten about all the suffering he had undergone.

As his general problems had now been solved, Deng had to care for us. He did not like that his friends were covered in dust and living in a school pantry. So he rented an entire two-story building that was owned by a close female friend.

We said goodbye to Comrade T., who had so graciously helped me as if she had been my sister, and to Wo, our dark-skinned Taiwanese friend. I prayed that they would continue to work fervently in the mutual love of comradery.

We would have said goodbye to Comrade R. too, but he was then at the university hospital. We visited him once there. He was less vigorous than before, but his cheeks were still rosy, and his gentle smile never left him. It seemed to me that he was suffering not only from an illness of the body, but one of the heart. When would he reunite with his dear Taiwanese lover? Poor soul! I said goodbye to the other students and goodbye to the building, which, despite its ruinous appearance, continued to burn bright with the life of youth.

Our roommates in our new lodging were Deng and another Esperantist—a poor, homeless student from Sun Yat-sen University. We affectionately called our nest the Green House, which was cleaned daily by one of those antimarriage "revolutionary women" of which I wrote earlier. As the Green House had several empty rooms, we invited Comrade Ye to stay with us if he could not involve us in the movement in Hankou and wanted to come work with us here in Guangzhou. The rooms could potentially serve other comrades passing through the city. Deng also intended to hold classes there. "However," he explained to us, "they must exclusively consist of women!"

The International Association of Guangdong

Once he knew he had to stay here for a sufficient time, a plan fixed itself in Ren's head: to produce international propaganda using Esperanto.

But how?

Over ten years prior, when Guangzhou was at its revolutionary apex, the Esperanto movement had enjoyed a flowering period. The mayor at the time was an Esperantist, and a lot of money was poured into the movement. However, as the saying goes, "Nothing lasts forever." Now only a small group of students, with no real influence in society, maintained the movement. Aside from them, Ren also knew some "Shanghai intellectuals" who might understand the significance and utility of Esperanto. But between them and the nationalist government, he could find no direct line.

Then Deng returned. He loved women, good food, new clothes, and comfortable lodgings. He also helped friends, loved justice, truth, action, and *revolution*. In a word, everything beautiful and good, for he was a typical youth. So he, Ren, and a few other friends quickly got down to business. Perhaps Deng paid a visit to one of his eminent relatives and acquaintances and explained the situation. I don't really know, for at the time I had to stay cooped up in the Green House.

The efforts paid off, and we founded the International Association of Guangdong under the aegis of the Guangdong government.

The task of the association was to produce international propaganda. It consisted of three departments, each organized around a different language: Esperanto, Japanese, and English. To the Japanese department—that is, the anti-Japanese department—we wanted to invite Kaji Wataru, who was still hiding out in Hong Kong along with his wife, Ikeda Yuki. However, the government denied our request. For them, Kaji was an unknown Japanese national, and they did not trust him. Moreover, Guangdong was far from the front and had only a local government. Therefore, from the start we did not have terribly high hopes that our work would get off the ground.

Before long, the English-language department folded.

Only the Esperanto department knew how to proceed. First, the majority of its members were Esperantists. Second, they were more or less experienced in the field of international propaganda. Every member of the Green House took part, myself included. So did Chen Yuan, the representative of the Guangdong Esperanto Association. We assembled a list of addresses of Esperantists and Esperanto groups located all over the world. The plan was to publish a monthly magazine, *Justeco*, which would provide information about the war in China. We would also make pretty medals on which were written the words *Amiko de Ĉinio* (Friend of China) and would publish political pamphlets, the first of which would be—as proposed by Ye Laishi from Hankou—a collection of my works, and those of Kaji, which I would translate. The comrades agreed to this proposal. It would be a quiet but righteous cry and call from the heart, which the Japanese people would not dare to speak in their own land. To the pamphlet we would give the title "The Japanese Are Speaking."

So flowered our Esperanto labors in Guangdong. However, I was beginning to get increasingly impatient. I was no anationalist, after all.[39] I was Japanese. So as a Japanese person living in China, I felt I had a special duty. When would I be allowed to

---

39. Anationalism: An antinationalist ideology closely associated with the ideas of the Esperantist Eugène Adam (a.k.a. Lanti, 1879–1947), the Sennacieca Asocio Tutmonda (World Anational Association), and the magazine *Sennaciulo* (Anationalist).

carry it out? All around me, people were speaking in a language I did not understand while on the street, curious eyes watched me or turned their heads to look at me with suspicion, although this no longer made me feel so uneasy or displeased.

Back the Way I Came

Every morning we went to the office, which was located not far from our place, next to several important institutions protected by armed guards.

One morning at the end of February, around two weeks after the establishment of our association, Wo Dan and I were on our way to the office as usual. The sun was shining brightly in the blue sky. There had been talk of an air strike. But out on the street, everything seemed to be completely ordinary.

An airplane droned low over our heads.

"Strange," Wo murmured. "Is it ours?"

It could not be the enemy. Why would it risk flying so low, and alone? Moreover, no alarm had been raised. To me, it was as if the airplane had always been above our heads, as if it had been following us around, like the illusion we experience on certain nights when the moon seems bent on following us wherever we go.

I felt a twinge of anxiety in my chest. Not from the airplane. It was in the sky and did not concern me on the ground. No, the anxiety was triggered by two men walking behind us. At first, I told myself that we were all simply taking the same street, so I intentionally slowed down my pace. Then they slowed down too.

There was no doubt about it....

Wo whispered to me in Esperanto: "Have you noticed that we're being followed?"

I nodded my head in silent assent. Of course I had noticed, but what could I do?

By now, the airplane had flown off and was barely audible. When I finally arrived at the office and my desk and was about to take up my pen, the two men entered and began talking with

Deng, Ren, and Chen, who were already there. They did not turn around once to ask me questions. It all resembled that day at the port and in the New Asia Hotel eight months before. But this time I could not hide my identity, nor did I need to. Had I not been allowed to join the propaganda department on the express knowledge that I was Japanese? Why, I had even seen my name on the members' register!

Suddenly, the word "airplane" brushed passed my ears.

Wait—had they actually said it, or had I merely misheard them? But what in the world did an airplane have to do with me? I had often heard that traitors would wave handkerchiefs and other things to direct enemy airplanes toward air-strike targets. Earlier, on the street, I myself had used a handkerchief two or three times to shield my eyes from the strong rays of the sun. Had they taken that as...Hah! What nonsense! Was I imagining things? That airplane had definitely been Chinese. Didn't they know that? But were they really talking about the airplane? Perhaps it was all in my head.

. . .

"Deportation!"

One simple word.

Deportation! It was not my imagination but a fact.

And to this was added two more words.

"Without delay."

. . .

On the following afternoon, I was sitting on a train to Hong Kong with Deng. Like other rich Cantonese people, his mother kept rooms in Hong Kong, for this "neutral" city was not threatened by enemy shelling.[40] For the time being, I would stay there and wait for Ren, who would come in two or three days. He had to make arrangements for everything. As he was Chinese, he was not being deported from the country. He could stay in Guangdong, the detectives said. That was the law after all. And yet, how

---

40. Hong Kong would later be invaded and occupied in December 1941.

could he let me go alone? Half of the Cantonese men who had Japanese wives had done so, including Mr. U., while the other half had taken refuge with their wives in the neutral zones. Certainly, they had been wiser than we. Why had we not stayed in Hong Kong months prior? Had we feared the expensive life and prying eyes of the Japanese? No, I believe that even if those things had not bothered us, we still would have risked everything coming to the heart of Fighting China. I did not want to wait out the war like my "sisters." I did not want to take their path. I had hoped and believed that, somehow, some day, we would surely overcome all obstacles before us.

I had hoped, and my dream had become a reality, if only partly... Leafing through the pages of the past, my memories suddenly came unbound and fell to the ground. Had any of it really existed? Was it all a dream?

The train raced along the rails.

The sun was beginning to set. Deng was silent, though his face was not altogether severe. I never imagined he could go so long without talking. At every station he disembarked to buy some small snacks and put them before me. Among them were what appeared to be black roasted insects, which elsewhere might have delighted children as playthings. To show my appreciation, I took some fruit and sweets. But I had no appetite. It was not the black insects that had robbed me of it. Deng, too, did not eat much.

How many more stations remained ahead? I had no idea. When we had come to Guangdong, we had come by ship. I did not ask Deng. After all, I felt completely indifferent to when we would arrive. Previously, I had told myself that I would not become like my Japanese "sisters." Now, whether I liked it or not, I was dragging myself along their gray and narrow path. But while they had gone ahead according to a plan, I was following them by accident. Consequently, that which was waiting for me at my final destination was really nothing.

A big, black nothing...

★

When did I fall asleep? I was woken by the sound of conversation. Beside me were two men in Western dress and behind them, an armed guard. They exchanged a few words with Deng in Cantonese. I didn't understand what they were saying but could guess at the meaning. In my head, there loomed the pale face of Comrade R.'s lover, though I had never seen her. Remember, I thought, bracing myself, she is Taiwanese, while I am Japanese! At last, it had come to pass, that which had threatened to come many times before. And yet this time I felt no fear, for my hatred and indignation for those who had taken this path exceeded it. I noticed the compartment was illuminated with electric lights. Was it their light that was making Deng look so pale?

"They are saying that we must return to Guangdong."

His tone was gentle. Surely he did not want to worry me. I nodded to him with a mixture of gratitude and apology.

We disembarked at the next station, which was lit by one thin lamppost. Already on the platform stood four armed guards. After a moment, the illuminated train sped away, leaving us in the half-light, waiting for somebody to take us back the way we came. The late February air was cold, and the guards' bayonets gleamed icily before us.

—the unfinished end—

Postscript

I did not intend, nor am I capable of, writing a novel or novella. This little work is but a collection of fragments from my time in China.

My seven years inside Fighting China can be split into three periods. The first was my drifting period, which began with my arrival in Shanghai and ended with my exile to Hong Kong. Driven by the one goal of participating in the War of Resistance, I spent over a year in hiding. Therefore, the first part of *Inside*

Fighting China had to be as you have read, though I did not want to give to it the character of an autobiography.

The second period was my Hankou period. Thanks to the efforts of my friends, on the eve of the first anniversary of the War of Resistance, I was granted permission to work in the anti-Japanese division of the Central Propaganda Department. This period hardly lasted three months, for in the middle of October we had to abandon Hankou, which fell on the twenty-sixth. How brief but exciting, invigorating but tiring it was! The passion of the people, the government, and the army reached its zenith; the cooperation between the KMT and the CCP was fully realized; the military resistance became national in the true sense of the word. In this part of my work, I planned to no longer write about myself and the small world around me. The things I saw, heard, and felt there are those I will never forget and, I imagine, would surely touch the hearts of righteous people everywhere.

The third period is my Chongqing period. It began in the winter of 1938 and will end who knows when. That first winter, the entire city was covered by a dense blanket of fog. One day, I half-jokingly asked my neighbor who had grown up in the city: "Is there no sun in Chongqing?" The good man seemed offended: "What do you mean? Of course, there's a sun! It's just hidden by the fog." And indeed, when spring finally arrived, the fog lifted, and we saw the sun radiating serenely in the blue sky. But strangely, we felt as if another gray and humid fog still surrounded us. Recently, in the world outside, there have been great strides toward the light, but this foggy city remains ever foggy. Beneath the fog I have seen many things that should have no place in Fighting China. The third part of the work I would dedicate to that, though, in all honesty, it pleases me not.

Such is my plan for *Inside Fighting China*. But already, when I have not even fully worked out the first part, I am faced with constant interruptions. Therefore, for the foreseeable future I will not be able to continue it. It is a shame that I cannot incorporate the second and third parts, which I feel are more significant.

My drifting life has slid far into the distance. Although it was difficult and uneasy, in my mind the picture I have of it is moving, nostalgic even. The Hankou period—which I do not limit to my short stay in Hankou but expand to the entire so-called stage of the war—is now a "rosy yesterday." Meanwhile, for the past five and a half years, we have been stagnating in this foggy city, often asking ourselves: "Is there no sun here?"

Is it true, what my neighbor had said, that the sun is only hidden by the fog? Perhaps it is so. But when, I wonder, will that fog fully lift?

Last, I would like to thank my Esperantist and non-Esperantist elders and friends, who have always supported me. Had it not been for your kindness, I cannot begin to imagine where and in what state I would be now.

VERDA MAJO
July 10, 1944
a village near Chongqing

2

TWO LOST APPLES

—from my sickbed—

SEATED ON OUR SUNNY VERANDA, I dutifully perform a monthly "special service" for my mother.

How strange—her white hairs, which ordinarily take me half an hour to remove, are today not decreasing at all. Rather, they seem to be increasing. Reflected in the mirror, my mother, looking utterly exhausted, maintains a lengthy silence.

"Little May..."

Then, in a harsh voice I have never heard before.

"Why have you lost those apples I so lovingly gave you?"

"Mummy..."

Embarrassed, I hold my pale cheeks in my hands.

"In Shanghai you could still find some apples. But not later, Mummy—not in Guangzhou, nor in Hankou, nor in Chongqing. So I ate mine."

My mother says nothing. I, too, speak not a word and continue my work. But the white hairs keep increasing. Now her whole head is almost white.

I exclaim, unable to bear it.

"Mummy!"

Nothing.

"Mummy, Mummy!"

Half in anger, half in jest, I grab her frail shoulders and look at her face.

Ah! It is not my mother but a statue of alabaster. Cold and frozen like ice...

I awake.

The inside of my brain throbs in pain; my chest is wet with oily sweat.

Here and there lamps flicker,
But only your window is dark
Like a lonesome blind eye—Why?
Mother—
Does the breeze of spring nights through green leaves
Not caress, with gentle freshness, your weary head?
Do the lilacs in the garden, white, even in darkness,
Not embrace, with sweet perfume, your weak body?

Oh, I know why.
Behind the firmly shut glass window,
Behind the heavy blue curtains,
You are turning the dial of the radio
With your veiny, trembling hand.
Your favorite violin performance now over.
Bzz-bzz-bzz, kssh-kssh-kssh.
A mishmash of sounds grates on your ears.
But soon—
Radio waves from across mountains of ocean
Carry to you a familiar voice.
The voice of your daughter, who flew away
Like a bird from your breast.

Every evening, when I stand before the microphone,
I am seized by an urge to cry: "Mummy!"
Some seething and heartrending feeling runs through me.
But a moment later, there appear before my eyes

Diverse and innumerable faces:
Sad, weary, hungry, angry, vengeful faces
Of men, women, children, and the elderly.

Mother!
My one and only mother, you are the most dear to me.
But I cannot be yours alone.
So do not tell me to enjoy my little happiness in secret,
in the middle of this cruel war,
in the middle of this storm of tears and sighs and curses.

"Shameless traitor!"—
The venomous tongues of fascist agents,
The malicious eyes of cruel and uneducated people,
Tortures your already weak heart.
But Mummy,
Open your eyes! Look at your Little May!
This love for the weak and the suffering,
This hatred for all tormentors,
This valorous "pride"—These things are treasures
You once gave to me—
Have I lost even one of them?
No, all that your daughter has lost, or had to lose,
Is the red of her cheeks.

Some weeks ago,
To search for my two lost apples,
I went to M Bathhouse.[1]
Sunlight was falling on the green earth;
Yellow rapeseed flowers stretched before me;
A sweet perfume of bright purple bean flowers

---

1. This may be a reference to the South Hot Spring in Chongqing, in which case the *M* would stand for "Minami" (meaning "South" in Japanese).

Thrilled me in my exhaustion.
"Why, is this not the Village of K,[2]
In which I spent my childhood?
The fields over which I pulled your sleeve,
Dancing and shouting at the top of my lungs:
'It's spring, it's spring'?"
Eternal paradise unknown to war!
I bid it farewell too early.
Was it memory that drove me away from there?

Drifting from north to south, from east to west,
For two long years,
The apples on my cheeks disappeared—
I'm sorry, Mummy, I don't know when or where it
    happened.
All that I know is that they were taken from me
By the same hateful hand
That took them away from hundreds of thousands,
From thousands of millions, of youths and children
In China and Japan, my homeland.

Now I—we,
Must take back what has been taken from us.
How can we obtain them?
By standing back and doing nothing?
Mother—
Do not shield your ears, do not cover your eyes,
Even from death.

It is only from the fiery crucible of battle
That we will be able to take them back.

---

2. Possibly a reference to Kashiwagi (now part of Shinjuku Ward), an area in Tokyo where Hasegawa spent some of her childhood. Alternatively, since Hasegawa made a conscious effort to avoid direct references to her family, *K* may refer to Yamaguchi, another childhood locale.

But Mother,
If your daughter should lose forever
Those apples that you so lovingly gave her,
Do not reproach her.
For they are only two of the innumerable apples,
Which had to fall before their time,
So that new apples might ripen, eternally beautiful,
On the mainland, in Japan,
And all over the wide world.

April 1939, Chongqing

3

MAY IN THE CAPITAL CITY

> May flowers bloom in the fields,
> over the blood of the patriots.
> In order to save our perilous nation,
> they fought to the very end.
>
> —"May Flowers"

BETWEEN THE TWO RIVERS...[1]

The sky is high and clear. Across its blue depths float white puffs of clouds.

Green leaves shine from the flatlands to the hills, through which snake stone walls, black and gray, and straw hats moving fast and slow.

Beloved mainland city, Chongqing!

I shall not sing to you a May pastoral. For though dressed in green, you, O heart of the great War of Resistance, are now burning with a fighting spirit. Moreover, this month, you have received the red baptism several times!

On the third, fourth, twelfth, and twenty-fifth...

There appeared in the sky a horde of silver-winged devils. *Boom! Boom! Boom!*

Epigraph: "May Flowers," a patriotic anti-Japanese song from 1936 with lyrics by Guang Weiran and set to music by Yan Shushi.

1. I.e., the Yangtze and the Jialing.

The earth bled beneath you, while above you burned the sky. And your people...

O, you are shaking your head! I can see that you do not want me to speak about the horrible tragedies unfolding before you.

Surely it is not I, a foreigner, but you yourself who suffers them most deeply.

You weep for the thousands of your dead, for still more orphans and widows.

You bemoan your broken arms, your burned legs.

You are covered in blood—yet you are not afraid.

Your blood-fearing parasites—the Wangists[2]—have fled from you, into the embrace of the bloodthirsty Japanese fascists!

Those traitors and aggressors must know that the threat of blood will never subjugate you, but rather gives you more fighting spirit.

For you, Chongqing, great mother of the New China, will endure any trial, always and by whatever means available to you.

May...

May in China, this semicolonized land, has a bloody history.

May 1—

Even in so-called independent and democratic nations, the working class cannot truly celebrate this day without the shedding of blood.

May 4, 1919: The day of the anti-imperial revolution, in which students from Beijing rebelled and rallied to punish the traitors to the nation.

May 7, 1915: The day on which the Japanese empire sent its fateful ultimatum to the reactionary militarist Yuan Shikai, then president of China, demanding the immediate and unconditional acceptance of the Twenty-One Demands of Japan.

---

2. Wangists: Supporters of Wang Jingwei. See chapter 1, note 17.

May 9, 1915: The day on which Yuan Shikai accepted the Japanese demands.

May 30, 1925: The day of the anti-imperial protest in Shanghai, which was a prelude to the great Chinese Revolution of 1925–1927.

May in China is referred to as "The Month of National Dishonor."

But know, my Chinese friends, that, despite their losses, your forebearers fought as bravely as you do now against the imperialists.

To remember them, you should rename May "The Month of Glory."

To avenge them, you must later make it the "The Month of Victory"!

May in Tokyo—

I cannot forget its special beauty after cherry-blossom season, for until the outbreak of the war, that is where I spent my impressionable childhood.

Time and time again, I was seized, as were my friends and comrades, by an inexpressible "melancholy of the green-leaf time."

O, for although in my homeland there raged no warplanes nor cannons, something else weighed heavily upon the hearts and minds of the people!

May in Hong Kong—

Resplendent, chiefly because of its "guaranteed peace."

I was there last year.

Yet how sad I was living there, for I had just been deported.

My beloved China had refused to accept me into her heart, and what's more I had no homeland to return to.

This year I find myself in the heart of Fighting China.

For the first time in my life I have known, and seen, how beautiful, how dear, is the Red May, O! to me, the Green May!

The "May Flowers" first bloomed in Manchuria and were a song sung as a prelude to the great "March of the Volunteers."

From then, they have bloomed nine times, more and more each year, from the distant northeast to here, in the southwest!

This month, the flowers turned red in Chongqing, but not on the bodies of the soldiers.

And next May?
O what is there to fear?
If necessary—
May the whole city bloom red, at any cost!
May all of China bloom red, all year round!

Soon the time will surely come...
When everywhere on this green continent...
Imbued with new life, May Flowers will smile.
Let them not drink blood in vain.

May 1939, Chongqing

Part 2

TO ESPERANTO LAND

4

LOVE AND HATE

THE INTERNATIONAL CITY is covered with smoke and fire.[1] From every street, there rises horrifying cries of terror and fear.

A cannon thunders, startling the still air of midday. Surely hundreds of men have fallen by now, some silently drawing their last breath, while the bloodied bodies of others writhe through the mud and the ruin.

On a blue canvas of sky—a silver warplane. Suddenly, it explodes and disappears, replaced by a few cloud-like masses.

Every impoverished quarter of the French Concession is overflowing with blackened refugees, like ants. Whatever street we walk down, begging hands reach out to us—be they withered, callused, or incredibly small.

"Who did this? The Japanese?"

"No!" I shake my head furiously, the entirety of my body responding with abhorrence. "It was the Japanese *imperialists!*"

At night I am wakened by the sound of gunfire. Unable to fall back asleep, I get out of bed and go to the balcony. The sky to the northwest is red. I tremble at its beauty. A fire there is burning as it had in 1932 and now threatens to consume not only Shanghai, Beijing, and Tianjin but all of China and its millennia-long

---

1. The international city: A reference to Shanghai.

culture, to which Japan's culture owes such an enormous debt. Given the right conditions, I imagine that the wind could blow this fire on and on until it had united with the fire of Spain, and from there the two fires would go on to envelop the world in one infernal flame.

Could things have been worse today?

I will never forget how those pillars of smoke also suffocate the people of Japan—land of the aggressor . . . and dear homeland of mine.

Before me I see the hopeless faces of workers bemoaning the inflating prices of everyday necessities; in my ears I hear the weeping of the elderly in the country and women robbed of their husbands and sons by war. Beneath this fire that is consuming Shanghai, I recall memories of my friends and family. . . .

I feel a sharp pain.

My heart weeps: no more war, for both peoples!

But is it a "false peace" that I desire, conditional on the continued humiliation of the Chinese nation? No! A hundred—a thousand times no! The Chinese will purchase back their freedom with their own flesh and blood. That said, they well know that "true peace" can only be achieved with the help of their Japanese brothers and sisters, and I am tormented by shame and anger, knowing that too few Japanese fight for that future. Under the almighty power of the state, the Japanese people are choosing to keep silent about the war. Is that not complicity, be it willful or not, with the inhuman aggressor?

News arrives—

"Japanese soldiers have refused to disembark from their transports, and will be forced to go ashore on the threat of death."

"One hundred Japanese and Chinese students have been shot to death for participating in antiwar demonstrations in Tokyo."

In my breast there blooms a blood-red rose. Surely this is an outpouring of the true and suppressed feeling of the Japanese people.

I love Japan, for it is my homeland. My parents live there, my siblings, relatives, and friends. It is a place full of happy memories.

I love China also, for it is my new homeland. Indeed, it is here that I am surrounded by many kind and hard-working comrades.

I hate—no, I despise the murderous warring between the two peoples. And if one of them were to die, I would drown in despair.

As an Esperantist, as a lover of the world's many cultures, I pray that Chinese culture will be spared from the aggressor's talons.

As a woman, as a human being, I instinctively yearn for peace.

But now, if possible, I would join the Chinese army, for it is fighting for the freedom of the Chinese nation, not against the Japanese people but the Japanese Empire, and its victory will lead to a bright future for all of East Asia.

So together with my comrades, I call out to my Japanese brothers: do not spill blood in vain; your enemy is not here across the sea!

August 1937, Shanghai

5

VICTORY FOR CHINA IS THE KEY TO TOMORROW FOR ALL OF ASIA
A Letter to Japanese Esperantists

COMRADES!

How long I have been silent! At first, it was the Japanese censors that made me hesitant about writing to you openly. And now, for over two and a half months, the war has prevented our correspondence. But I can no longer hold myself back. Indeed, some powerful, complicated feeling compels me to write to you....

But where shall I begin?

Comrades! Whatsoever nation one may belong to, he who has a human heart and clear reason must sympathize with China. I am not some senseless beast. I know a thing or two about justice. That is why the same question has occupied my mind for so long now: "What should I do?" Should I go to the front like some of my male comrades, or should I take care of refugees and wounded soldiers like the women? I am afraid I can do neither, for I am a weak woman who cannot even speak proper Chinese. But comrades! Fortunately, I am an Esperantist. I write "fortunate," for due to this fact I have found my calling in this revolutionary struggle against the imperialists. At last, the time has come to use our language more effectively as an international weapon. "For China via Esperanto!" is not just a pretty phrase on paper. My work with

Ĉinio hurlas and other such magazines is not confined to contributing my miserable technique as a foreign Esperantist to help produce some flimsy rag. Whenever I take up my pen, my blood boils at the oppression of justice, and a fiery rage is stoked against the brutish enemy. I rejoice: I am with the Chinese people!

Call me a traitor, if you wish! I am not afraid. Rather, I am ashamed to belong to a nation that has not only invaded another but is carelessly creating a living hell for innocent and helpless refugees. True patriotism does not stand in the way of progress. If it did, it would be chauvinism. And how many chauvinists has the war produced in Japan! I could scarcely hold back my anger and disgust when I heard how intellectuals who had once claimed to be conscious, progressive, even Marxist, are now shamelessly following reactionary militarists and politicians, beating the drum for "the just cause" of the imperial army. Murofuse Kōshin, a critic with a large influence on the intelligentsia, boasts of Japan's mission to create a new world order, any opposition to which must perish, and that is his reasoning for why the present war is fated for the two great nations of the East. Meanwhile, Yamakawa Hitoshi, previously a scientific socialist, has put forward a specious argument about the supposed "diabolic brutality" of the Chinese army and indignantly calls the Chinese people "more fiendish than beasts." ... Ah, but surely you know more about that than I.

Oh comrades, how can one so easily discard one's last shred of conscience? Yet I believe in you and remain certain that you will not take even one step toward them, for only you, progressive Esperantists, true internationalists, can fully comprehend the significance of this war and the correct course of action to take.

Between China and Japan there exists no fundamental hatred. On the contrary, leaf through the annals of history, and you will find amicable relations on every page. During the 1911 Xinhai Revolution, many Japanese willingly spilled their blood for their neighbor's freedom. And just a few years ago, how firmly did the workers of both nations join hands for the emancipation of the proletariat! Comrades, I can clearly recall the enthusiasm with which we spoke about this in Tokyo, how earnestly we discussed efforts to have Japanese and Chinese Esperantists cooperate to accelerate the movement, first in the East and then throughout the wide world. Last spring, prior to my departure from Japan, this goal became particularly urgent. But then various factors—the greatest among them being suppression by the Japanese police—prevented it from becoming a reality.

Comrades, the time has come! We urgently need your help. The Chinese people require all manner of support. How could you forsake them now? Indeed, today affords a golden opportunity to take the first step in a lengthy and significant project, to take direct and meaningful action. A little hesitation will cause much regret for you, and shame for us. Thorny will be the path, a fact we knew from the start. But what does that matter? Comrades, know that in spite of the government's threats, antiwar protests are currently simmering or breaking out all over Japan. Even Japanese soldiers in Shanghai are putting up antiwar posters at the risk of severe military punishment!

Comrades, China's victory in this war will lead not only to the liberation of the Chinese nation but also to the liberation of all the oppressed nations of the Far East, including Japan! Indeed, its victory is the key to tomorrow for all of Asia—if not the key to tomorrow for all of the world. How could we allow ourselves to waver? Mind you that any refusal to act now will henceforth be considered an admission of your guilt. However, I need not waste my breath on that, for I have complete faith in your unwavering support.

Oh comrades! If only you could see how heroically and resiliently the Chinese soldiers are fighting at this critical stage of the war! Often does it make my heart beat fast and fill my eyes with tears. If only you yourselves could see them.... Meanwhile, how pitiful are the soldiers of our native land. Why, just last week the newspapers reported that more than twelve thousand Japanese soldiers had perished in Shanghai. And now the government is

Victory for China Is the Key to Tomorrow 119

shipping over thousands upon thousands of young persons to take their place. How can I know that one of you will not be found among them? No! The mere thought of this terrifies me. To go to war with one's oppressed neighbor and die in vain... Tell me, is there a greater tragedy for us Esperantists?

Till our next correspondence,

Wishing a good fight and good health to you all!

September 1937, Shanghai

6

TO ALL THE ESPERANTISTS OF THE WORLD

DEAR COMRADES!

Today is the birthday of our esteemed Dr. L. L. Zamenhof, who, from childhood, fought tirelessly to establish a sense of brotherhood among every nation and peace for all mankind but sadly breathed his last breath amid the wholesale world butchery of men by fellow men. In remembering this hallowed anniversary while an all too similar terror is presently unfolding across China, I am seized by inexpressible pain. I am Japanese, true, but I am also a friend of the Chinese people, and even their fellow combatant. That is why I cannot stop myself from writing to you today, dear adepts of peace.

But first some greetings:

Spanish comrades—Comrade Mangada and others now fighting against the fascists of Germany, Italy, and their Francoist agents; comrades from *Popola fronto* and *Informacio;* and all comrades of the popular front...[1]

---

1. Julio Mangada (1877–1946): An Esperantist and prominent Spanish Republican Army officer. *Popola fronto* and *Informacio* were Esperanto magazines published by the Popular Front.

German comrades—Comrade Renn, now fighting in Madrid; comrades suffering in Hitler's prisons; and those fighting "Germany over all" by way of secret radio broadcasts and other means, despite suppression and terror...[2]

Soviet comrades—you who have endured one hardship after another and now, in embarking on the most extensive mission to improve all aspects of social life, are showing the way to tomorrow for Esperantists everywhere....

Japanese comrades—dear comrades from home, with whom I once worked and who, though fallen silent, are doubtless, in one way or another, struggling against the invasion in the face of unprecedented suppression....

Comrades of the world—you who are standing alongside the forces of peace and are fighting against the forces of fascism...

I heartily salute you!

Behold, comrades! In the West, the demonic hands of the Italian and German fascists are furiously strangling the revolutionaries of Spain. Hitler continues his massacre of the Jews, is extending his talons over Austria, and has wrestled territory from Czechoslovakia. In the East, their bloodthirsty brothers, the Japanese militarists, have, for eighteen months now, trampled the vast earth and multitudinous people of China. The specter of a new world war is haunting the globe and threatens the whole human race.

Last autumn I witnessed the storming of Zhabei—people and homes, earth and sky, everything and anything, burned for over three days and nights. Last spring in Guangzhou, a densely populated city in southern China, I survived a terrible air strike. Some dozen Japanese warplanes madly shelled the city five or six

---

2. Ludwig Renn (1889–1979): The pen name of Arnold Friedrich Vieth von Golssenau, a German author and Esperantist who fought in the International Bridges during the Spanish Civil War and was a founding member of the International Association of Revolutionary Esperantist Writers (IAREV).

times a day. Wounded men suffocated under crumbling homes. On the streets there lay bodies, scattered arms and legs, women and children—even a small newborn, wrenched from its mother's womb prematurely by shelling. Guangzhou, once beautiful and prosperous, was transformed into a ruin, and above it shone the moon, a terror for survivors.

Screams, cries, and moans of orphans, widows, and the elderly…starving, cold, and homeless refugees growing in number by the hour.…This is the holy result of the "holy war" being waged by the Japanese militarists.

And in many cities and villages, the very same horror was repeated, is being repeated, and will be repeated.

And in the war zones and occupied territories?

European journalists have brought to your attention every kind of demonic act of violence wrought by the Japanese army. On my honor and love for the human race, I can attest to those facts. How terrible it is!

Comrades, forgive me if I am interrupting you at breakfast or while you are listening to music. I am trying to restrain my anger. But I must speak out. Believe me when I say that these crimes are being committed: Japanese soldiers raped a woman and cut off her breasts. They did not spare her ten-year-old daughter.

Comrades, believe me when I say that these crimes are being committed: Japanese soldiers are robbing children from their mothers' breasts and making them playthings of the devil. The children burst into tears, wailing loudly, uncontrollably, until at last their little hearts are pieced through with a sharp sword.

Comrades, believe me when I say that these crimes are being committed: Healthy, cherub-cheeked boys are being taken away and drained of their blood to treat wounded soldiers. Left barely alive, they are shoved into bags and thrown into rivers and marshes. (How many small corpses fill the Yangtze!)

Once in a prisoner-of-war camp, I encountered two Manchurians, one of whom was only capable of uttering groans, while the other had a limited vocabulary, like that of a paralytic. We learned from the latter that the Japanese militarists had given them special injections to silence their tongues and make them fight against their own brothers (after all, they were really Chinese and had only been taught to think of themselves as "Manchurians" by the invaders). I also encountered some young Korean girls, who in the name of "comfort" had been forced to satisfy the beastly desires of Japanese soldiers. Two of the girls were thin and jaundiced. A third was visibly suffering from an intense case of syphilis. And the rest all had round bellies—the devil only knows who the fathers were.

Comrades, believe me when I say that these crimes are being committed.

This is the "culture" of the imperial army in China. And under the hoofs of this culture, the trees of Mount Zijin have lost their green leaves, their branches and trunks burned to ash, and the once serene West Lake rages blood red.

The Chinese people love peace and stability and have five thousand years of invaluable culture behind them. They enjoy their work and take satisfaction in their harvests. From China's peaceful agrarian social order, which is symbolized by its vast green fields and quiet azure lakes, there have emerged great philosophies, poets, and politicians. Recently, its people have begun to march toward a new system of governance, democracy, striving to make their nation the happiest on Earth. But then the Japanese imperialists arrived. They not only forbid China from carrying on its brilliant traditions but are actively working to sever them by the bayonet, and moreover, in fabricating the most shameful lies, are trying to justify the barbarous crimes that they themselves are guilty of committing.

The same terror has been raging in Spain for two and a half years. Who knows if tomorrow it will be over your heads!

Right now, as I am writing to you, Japanese, German, and Italian fascists are marching hand in hand to threaten the culture of the human race and peace in the world. Tell me, does that not concern you as you strive to build your paradise on earth? The whole world has been split into two large and absolute factions: one of friendship and one of aggression. There is no need for me to state again to which side we must belong. And a neutral position is completely untenable. How could you, my fellow combatants for peace, fall silent during such pressing times as these? Is the green star still shining on your breast? If its light is to exist in the world, then the day has come to fight.

Since the outbreak of the war, Chinese Esperantists from diverse camps have united to increase their strength. Even those who had long abandoned the movement have returned to it once more with renewed enthusiasm, though they will have to overcome many difficulties to advance their project of spreading Esperanto.

Present circumstances have made our normally passive approach totally unacceptable. Comrades from the UEA and IEL, SAT and IPE—be you social democrats or anarchists—do you really intend to continue bickering over petty differences, thereby postponing our unification?[3] Disorganization holds us back while spurring on the ruination of mankind and an end to peace. Once again I reiterate: We have but one enemy: the fascists. These fascists will use any means, even Esperanto, to deceive and blind the world. Under the leadership of Dr. Fujisawa Chikao, a former professor of the Imperial University and member of the National Spiritual Culture Research Institute, reactionary Esperantists in Tokyo have established a state-funded Esperanto association that shamelessly howls to the world about the "righteousness" of Japan's aggression. To the same end, an Esperanto group in Wakayama publishes a monthly, *La suno*, which it distributes freely to a dozen different countries. In Kyoto, the well-established *Tempo* magazine has lowered the old standard of bourgeois liberalism to raise a new one of fascism. Comrades, can our Esperantist beliefs permit such dishonor? Esperanto was once the

---

3. UEA: Universal Esperanto Association; IEL: International Esperanto League; SAT: World Anational Association; IPE: International of the Proletarian Esperanto Movement.

language of Rolland, Gorky, and Marx! Comrades, can we really allow ourselves to hand our language over to the agents of fascism, to our executioners? Oh, comrades, this is why we must unite! This is why we must strike at the fascists and tear off their masks. Do not forget that Esperanto can serve as a powerful weapon against the barbarous destroyers of culture and universal peace so long as it maintains a strong international league. Remember that this weapon transcends all borders, that our comrades are everywhere, and that our voice can reach any corner of the globe. Being as we are at the vanguard of peace, we Esperantists have a duty to keep growing our united front until it is on a truly international scale, until it includes even the vast non–Esperanto-speaking community.

To this end, we must:

1. Establish and strengthen an antifascist united front of Esperantists.
2. Root out fascist Esperantists from our ranks.
3. Use Esperanto to make international propaganda against aggression.
4. Grow our united front beyond ourselves.

These are some proposals that I submit to you on the grand occasion of our dear leader's birthday. Indeed, I firmly believe that there is no better way to commemorate this year's Zamenhof Day than to realize them.

But before concluding, I would like to devote a few words to the present state of the War of Resistance now unfolding in China.

The War of Resistance is entering a new stage. The astonishing unification of the Southwest and Northwest, presently the heart of Fighting China, is advancing. Centuries ago, the Chinese nation erected its Great Wall. Today it adds to that the unrivaled unity of its people. No difficulty can overcome it. Cooperation between the Kuomintang and the Communist Party, as well as close ties between the people and the army, are growing stronger by the day. See how the vanguard of the Japanese army was successfully routed by guerillas who have come to play such an important role at this new stage. But I hear you: Had China a sufficient number of surface-to-air missiles or warplanes, the victims in our rear guard would not be so many. How pitifully our soldiers fall from a lack of gas masks! How many wounded suffer helplessly or die from a lack of medical supplies and nurses! And yet I do not doubt that even without any outside help, and in spite of ever-increasing difficulties, China will continue to resist and obtain its final victory. However, to help it is the duty of peace-loving people of every land, for the Chinese nation fights not only for its freedom but also for the peace of mankind. That is why I, a Japanese person in China, urge you to do the following. To fulfill these tasks is the duty of all Esperantists and every human being.

1. Call on your country to trigger Article 16 of the Covenant of the League of Nations.
2. Demand your government to forbid the export of military weapons to Japan.
3. Boycott Japanese goods.
4. Urge your people to send medical supplies, necessary goods, and money to China.

With a warm handshake,
Your comrade, Verda Majo
December 1938, Chongqing

7

IF WINTER COMES, CAN SPRING BE FAR BEHIND?

A letter to Comrade Mangada

WHY IS IT THAT I, a Japanese woman, find myself thinking about you, a Spanish general?

Is it love? Yes, if by "love" is meant the green love of Esperanto....

My memory races back three years.

December in Tokyo is gray and cold. And that year, especially so. The masses were oppressed by an atmosphere of "national crisis," trembling as if some enemy from across the sea were about to invade. The first storm against the young popular front raged across the nation, taking some of our best comrades.

On the fifteenth, as always, Esperantists celebrated Zamenhof Day. Strains of *Taigo* and *La espero* rang out under bright lights while our eminent members delivered speeches fervently praising the doctor's linguistic genius and glorifying his spirit of *homaranismo*.[1] At the same time, everybody was turning

---

1. The doctor: That is, Dr. L. L. Zamenhof, the inventor of Esperanto. *Homaranismo* (humanitism): A philosophy invented by L. L. Zamenhof based on the so-called golden rule (i.e., that one should treat others as one would like to be treated). An extension of Zamenhof's "internal idea" of Esperanto, it currently has less of a presence in the language than it did in the early twentieth century.

away from the cruel reality. Nobody dared to discuss Esperanto, fascism, and war in the same breath. It was as if they had completely forgotten about the plight of our Spanish comrades, who, with their guns and their pens, were actively fighting for national liberation and world peace.

My heart seethed with indignation. On my way home, I imagined telegraphing you at the front, to express our sympathy and comradery. Of course, I knew that warring Spain prohibited telegrams in foreign languages. But Esperanto is no foreign language! Not at all! On my lips there played an impish grin.

What a girlish fantasy!

Now I find myself in China, on the bloody earth, which is like that of your native land. I must confess that we young Esperantists in enfettered Japan envied the Esperanto squad Antaŭen of the International Brigade, which fought alongside the Spanish people. Even now does my heart fly to the front and back while I remain behind. Am I a coward, or too weak to carry a gun? All I can say is that I have grown somewhat, at least compared to who I was before. And so, dear comrade, I have begun to know the naked truth.

Madrid has fallen!

Comrade, I want you to know that on that day, here in the Far East, we Chinese and antifascist Japanese also firmly swore to continue fighting until our final victory against the common enemy of mankind.

Yet pain and anxiety torment me. How are you and your comrades holding up? Tell me, have you taken refuge somewhere, or have you had the misfortune of being thrown into some black concentration camp?

It could be that you are already....

You once jokingly wrote: "In terms of life and death, I am

like the almighty Jesus Christ, for I have died many times, and yet I live."

Let that be true once more!

Today is the eve of yet another Zamenhof Day.

In my mind, I wander through his native Poland.

For it was there that he once witnessed children of the same Mother Nature murdering each other because of a czarist policy that incited hatred among the peoples of different races. And he belonged to the most suffering people, the Jewish people! To think that he perished during the First World War, trembling under cannon fire, his heart breaking asunder as he watched the unraveling of all his hopes and dreams. And now, once again, blood is being spilled there, thanks to the imperialist powers of the world. Indeed, Poland has become a hotbed for the second World Butchery. I wonder: if the doctor were to come back to life, would he, like before, lament the storm outside his little cabin, not knowing what to do? No! Absolutely not! His heart was too human to rot as a "peaceful fighter" at a time like this. Indeed, I believe it would be your bloodied and callused hand that he would first reach out to and grasp firmly with his own, big and warm.

In the West, the fascists are scheming with provocation and intrigue, and the so-called democratic nations, by a wolfish display of "nonintervention" that has led to your temporary failure, have finally taken off their masks. Meanwhile, in the East the Japanese executioners carry out their shameless mission.

December in this mountain city is foggy and disquieting. For more than a week, my sickbed has not once been visited by sunlight. But I do not feel an ounce of sadness or despair. Rather, it is the fire of a new fighting spirit that stirs my feverish body. Filled with joy and pride, I declare that the Chinese people will never bow to violence, that Chinese Esperantists will never betray the shining star on their breasts!

Last, to you, my dear, respected friend, I dedicate this much-loved verse:

If Winter comes, can Spring be far behind?[2]
Ah, but where art thou now, O green knight of ours?

December 1939, Chongqing

---

2. Hasegawa is quoting from the last line of Percy Bysshe Shelley's "Ode to the West Wind."

8

ESPERANTO AND DEMOCRACY

WHAT DID THE IMPRESSIONABLE YOUNG ZAMENHOF SEE in czarist Russia? Privileges for the Great Russians, oppression for other peoples, pogroms for the Jews, and disenfranchisement for all, including some Great Russians. How different was this from the actions taken by the German and Japanese aggressors? In the heart of Zamenhof there raged a fury against despots and butchers, as well as a desire for peace and the creation of a universal family. So he created Esperanto, hoping that it might be used to bring equality and independence to all nations, big and small, strong and weak.

From its beginning, Esperanto has been naturally democratic and antifascist, though such expressions were not used at the time. How crooked it would have been had it not been allowed to follow a democratic path! Fortunately, the wise and caring Zamenhof declared early on that he was only its creator and, claiming no rights or privileges over it, gave his language to the people using it and let them develop it.

Indeed, Esperanto is not the property of Zamenhof, but of mankind. One need not, must not, blindly adhere to its vocabulary and style. Esperanto is not Russian nor English, nor is it European. It is international. Therefore, we eastern Esperantists also have a right and duty to advance it. In fact, it is what we have been doing all along.

There are many who have mocked Esperanto's spirit of *homaranismo* for its "utopian" character. And yet if one were to try to build the Esperanto movement without this spiritual foundation, it would end up being nothing more than a mirage. Really, what humane person would oppose the spirit of *homaranismo?* Behold, with each passing day the situation is becoming more and more unprofitable for the fascists. Surely you have not forgotten those magnificent words spoken at that conference of British, American, and Soviet representatives: "After the war, the world shall be like one democratic family." So claimed the most powerful politicians living today! *Homaranismo* is not democracy in one nation but democracy among all nations throughout the world.

Esperanto is democratic at its core. That is why the Hitlerites hate it so. After they have been destroyed—and this war is finally over—our democratic Esperanto will at last find fertile ground in a democratic world and will grow faster and richer. Realizing this, however, will require our constant effort, for no victory ever came of itself.

November 1943

9

THE MISFORTUNE OF A DEMOCRATIC WORLD

"I WAS SEIZED BY A STRANGE FEELING when I heard the Japanese language flowing from my children's mouths as if it were entirely natural," remarked Mr. S., a famous writer who brought his family to Chongqing from Shanghai last year.

I have experienced something similar. Not long ago, I met some young people from "Manchuria" and was surprised to find that they could speak Japanese as though it were their mother tongue. But in all truth, this was not very surprising at all, for it had been thirteen years since the Manchurian Incident. And so, from elementary school all the way to university, these youths had received a systematic education from their Japanese oppressors and, upon arriving in China, realized with great regret that their capacity to speak the national language was far below the level of the general populace.

This problem is more serious in Korea and Taiwan, which unlike "Manchuria" and Nanjing are not even nominally "independent." For this reason, most of the new generation of Koreans and Taiwanese do not know their mother tongue.

Although I cannot speak for certain about lands occupied by Hitler's army, the situation there may be the same. The fascists will not rest until they have achieved complete supremacy: not only militarily, politically, and economically but also culturally and ideologically. Language policy holds an important place in their agenda.

Since the Lugou Bridge Incident, the Japanese government has financially supported the creation of some Esperanto propaganda to justify the "righteousness" of their invasion. However, this does not mean that the fascists actually approve of Esperanto. Rather, they are using it for their own hypocritical end. The international language and fascism are two opposing ideas that cannot be reconciled in any way. In "Manchuria," the government proudly speaks of "harmony among the five nations," and at some universities, Japanese, Chinese, Koreans, Mongolians, and White Russians study and even live together. As for whose language they speak commonly among themselves, one need not ask. Would anyone dare raise the matter of an international language here?

Every fascist believes that their language will one day be the world's language. And that will happen if their ambition to dominate the world is realized. But humankind cannot allow this to take place. By the red blood in its veins, it is proving that such a project, such an ambition, is but the fantasy of barbarians.

Therefore, the approaching San Francisco Congress symbolizes a knockout blow by the democratic camp against the fascist horde. Among the forty nations to be gathered there are nations both large and small, strong and weak. Several were able to rise from under the invaders' hooves thanks to the help of the Allied armies. In many ways, the relations between the different nations are exceedingly complicated. But among them are no victors and vanquished, nor masters and slaves. Rather, democracy—*that* is the single authority that presides and rules over everything and everyone at the congress.

Representatives from forty nations will gather. This inevitably brings to mind the age-old "language problem." While English is undoubtedly understood by the majority of those who will be present, the "majority" is not "all." And this "majority" is greatly reduced if we limit it to those who can clearly express their ideas in the language. Suppose an Ethiopian representative wishes to speak in his own language: his words must be interpreted into forty other languages in order to be fully understood. What a waste of time and effort! Besides, this is not even possible. In the heads of our famous politicians, soldiers, and diplomats, the language problem never seems to come up. And if it does, it comes only as an afterthought. The times require them to consult on other more important and pressing matters. If the future of humanity were to be decided by congresses and bigwigs alone, we would no longer cite the need for an international language. However, the new world is democratic; it belongs to the people. In truth, the San Francisco Congress is nothing but a symbol of the people's struggle and will. Those attending are its representatives.

Indeed, this century is for the people. Not only domestic but also international matters will be decided by the people. And the people do not want to force their language on others, nor do they want to express themselves in another's tongue. They see no reason to oppose a neutral and democratic language that is easy to learn.

Esperanto was, is, and will, in all likelihood, always be seen as a utopian ideal. Every ideal suffers when taken for a fantasy by arrogant "realists" with narrow views. We never dream that one day any government would declare the full acceptance of Esperanto. This is why the people must fight in order to get what they want to enjoy.

Freedom given is not true freedom.

So long as the whole world is drenched in blood, the green star cannot shine. So let us continue in our efforts. Can democrats really ignore the language problem while fascists zealously satisfy their own language policies? The lack of a neutral international language is a misfortune for a democratic world. France, Hungary, Czechia, nations in which the Esperanto movement flourished before Hitler's invasion, are now coming back to life. Soon our comrades there will participate once again, if they have not already sacrificed themselves in battle against the barbarous Nazis or else have been cruelly slaughtered by them. Surely during those dark and painful days, they did not lose their faith in Esperanto but rather empowered it.

April 10, 1945

Part 3

ON FASCIST JAPAN

10

JAPAN—A NATION UNDER BARBAROUS RULE

DOES MY TITLE SEEM TOO HOSTILE TO YOU? Well, it is an ironclad fact. A Japanese myself, I have studied with my own eyes the methods of this barbarous police state, my homeland, and am not at all ashamed to say such things about it. Rather, I want to tell how my brothers and sisters are suffering daily from its oppression.

Hitler burns books unfavorable to him, and his ally, the Japanese government, has long acted similarly, only not with fire. Although the Japanese people are still developing their own modern culture, the government has cooked up a system of "Public Order and Good Morals" that hinders the influence of modern life. To date, this has often resulted in farces that expose the government for its utter incivility.

Ten or so years ago, the police decided to cut, without allowance, every artistic presentation of kissing or hugging from European films. Prior to that, they had tried to forbid the public exhibition of artistic nudes. Naturally, as people had already grown accustomed to seeing such works, they had to leave them be, though, on at least one occasion, were kind enough to throw a cloth over the private part of an innocent little nude sculpture!

And yet the Japanese like to boast to curious Europeans what national treasures are the works of our feudal period, a time when people painted portraits of licentious prostitutes. Today, if lovers, or married couples even, walk hand in hand (another European influence) at night in more or less unpeopled places, the police question them, or take them in. Ah, but nobody dares touch that abhorrent custom practiced in one village or another called "night crawling," whereby, after the autumn harvest, unmarried men engage in a half-public sex orgy that makes a "Virgin Mary" of many an unsuspecting young woman.[1]

This is how the Japanese ruling class defends "the public order and good morals of a nation with a sacred three-thousand-year history"!

And since the outbreak of the war?

The more brutal our fascist regime becomes, the more ingrained this system will be, all in the name of the "spiritual mobilization." I will now share with you a few bizarre examples of what this spiritual mobilization entails.

The Banning of Christmas

The authorities have banned Christmas, calling it "anti-Japanese" despite its being no different from other Japanese festivities.

Before the order was handed down, the management of the Imperial Hotel, whose main patrons are foreigners, declared: "As we have fulfilled our mission to introduce Christmas to Japan, we shall no longer celebrate it."

In times like these, it seems more important to curry favor with the state than to provide service to foreigners. Or do people fear a recurrence of that terror of Christmas 1931, the year of the

---

1. Night crawling: A reference to the Japanese custom of *yobai*. It was once common all over Japan, though the custom varied from place to place, and continued to be practiced in some rural areas into the twentieth century.

Manchurian Incident, when fascist mobs invaded several dance halls in Tokyo and threw excrement on the partygoers?

The Closure of Dance Halls

Late last year, the government threatened to close all fifty-two of our dance halls, their existence deemed detrimental to the morals of the nation, chiefly those of the Japanese family, and a hindrance to its spiritual mobilization.

Thrown into an existential panic, the proprietors of said dance halls proposed improvements to their venues and their dancers' behavior, improvements that would be appropriate for Japan and the current situation. To this end, they reintroduced traditional Japanese words for "dance hall" and "dancer" in place of their loanword counterparts, made their dancers join the Patriotic Women's Association and the Women's League for National Defense and forbid them from getting electric perms, and moreover, added patriotic marches to their One-Step dance repertoire.

What *should* have been outlawed, I think, were the cafés (which in Japan are not places for simply drinking coffee), geisha houses, and other brothels, including the world-famous pleasure quarters! Really, must we always hold onto the pleasure quarters as a symbol of "national pride" while denying dance halls for their mere foreignness? But on this point, Professor Fujisawa, a member of the Research Institute for National Spirit and Culture, can provide us with a philosophical explanation: "The concept of public service is an integral part of the Japanese spirit. It is, in fact, far more integral than the concept of self-sacrifice is to the European."[2] Aha, I see now—so prostitution is, in fact, the very embodiment of our culture of public service!!

---

2. Fujisawa Chikao (1893–1962): A polyglot, political scientist, and prominent Esperantist. Although once a vocal supporter of the League of Nations, he later turned to Fascist Italy and Nazi Germany as inspiration for reforming internationalism and began promoting fascist-influenced conceptions of Zen Buddhism and Shintoism in support of the Japanese Empire.

The Banning of Electric Perms

The reason for this surprising decree is that electric perms are allegedly contrary to Japanese manners and customs. It would appear our most eminent scholars believe that the natural beauty of a Japanese woman's hair is best represented by the *shimada, maru-mage,* or some other monstrous style of traditional coiffure by which the center of one's poor head is tortured to near baldness and decorated with false hair extensions that are made to stand up with an unhealthy dousing of oil!

The Banning of Mixed-Sex Education

Even today, outside of elementary schools, Japanese women are generally not allowed to be educated alongside the men. For in our land of male supremacy, they are seen not as human beings or members of society but only as servants for their husbands and providers for their children and are solely raised to be "good wives and wise mothers." Recently, a bill was put forward in the Diet to ban mixed-sex education for the small number of girls who continue on to high school on the basis that it "masculinizes the girls and ruins the fairer attributes that are proper to the Japanese female sex."

In addition to introducing mandatory crew cuts for middle-school boys, our benevolent authorities have sought to tighten extracurricular control over them, forbidding them from visiting shops, the cinema, culture cafés, and other such places without the presence of an accompanying adult. Thus, the city has been divided into sectors, and teachers, with the help of the police, are made responsible for every action of the students in their sector. One reason for this is that, in cities like Tokyo, young people play an important role in the antiwar movement and are often arrested for their participation.

Japan—A Nation under Barbarous Rule   143

★

This is how the ruling class hounds the population to return to Japan's "true self" and parrot slogans of national chauvinism and spiritualism. But when all is said and done, what do the Japanese really have to be proud of as their own? Because of its lack of natural resources, Japan can support no kind of heavy industry without the importation of raw materials. Moreover, it is similarly impoverished in terms of culture. Does the ruling class not see that by doing away with all European influence, they are causing the ruin of modern Japanese social life? Surely in this they dare to show us their rare talent of knowing how to destroy, but not to build. Or do they wish to perform a grotesque skeleton dance, whereby they seek to exhume everything from the past?

If electric perms and dances are to be forbidden for being anti-Japanese, then every official should tear off his European uniform at once, and Prime Minister Konoe and other high-ranking officials should stop playing golf. In fact, why bother using cannons and airplanes, which the Japanese once referred to as "cowardly flying warships"? We therefore sincerely recommend the following to the government: "Arm your soldiers with Japanese swords, the manifestation of your beloved samurai spirit, and you will no longer need to cry so hoarsely from the altar to continue your "holy war."

May 1938, Hong Kong

11

AN AGE OF SUBSTITUTES— VIGNETTES OF WARTIME JAPAN

1. Wartime Regression

My train arrived in Tokyo.

I ran outside, hoping to go home by taxi. I had been away from my parents for two long years. But what the devil! Instead of the taxis that I had known to always swarm before the station, I found nothing but dirty rickshaws.

The rickshaw I hailed slowly carried me from street to street, so slowly, in fact, that I feared the rickshaw driver might be hungry or ill....

So many getas![1] I could hardly believe my eyes. Even men in modern European suits were clattering with them against the pavement. Some fifty years before, a fanatic lover of Japan by the name of Lafcadio Hearn had wondered at the wooden sound of getas as one of "Japan's mysteries." Did the Japanese government now intend to parade this national product before the world? But oh! Everybody knows that warring Japan no longer has leather for

---

1. Geta: Traditional Japanese footwear with a flat wooden base set upon two or three risers.

144

An Age of Substitutes—Vignettes of Wartime Japan   145

shoes, and even Hearn, were he to suddenly rise up from the grave, would shake his head in utter dismay at this anachronism.

When I stopped in Shinjuku to change rickshaws, I heard a radio loudspeaker exclaim: "Attention: Mr. Ikeda Nariaki, the minister in charge of wartime rationing, has just requested a carriage with a coachman. Attention..."

2. The New Moral

Mother is sad. Though her daughter has returned, she is weeping for her son on the Chinese battlefield and grumbles about the rising cost of goods and taxes. She complains that the hospital gives her ineffective medication, that she has to eat whale meat instead of beef and pork, that her false gold teeth were taken out and replaced with some kind of alloy that made all food more or less inedible, et cetera, et cetera.

But mostly she is upset about "S.F."[2] "How unpleasant it is on the skin, how flimsy, and, moreover, how expensive! For the women of the Patriotic Women's Association and the Women's League for National Defense, an apron made of S.F. can always be white and perfect. But what about working women? I have to buy at least two for the maid each month. And it's the same for kimonos and tabi socks. Imagine, so many expenses! Surely the Chinese also use this dreaded S.F., or perhaps something worse?"

"No," I responded straightaway. "They have cotton."

"China is a country of 'haves,'" interjected my father, "while Japan is a country of 'have-nots.' This is the cause of the war."

I would have refuted this fascist explanation had my mother not piped up again.

"I went to Izu the other day. And I don't know what kind of hot spring I soaked in, but would you believe it, my S.F. towel just dissolved in the bath, and..."

---

2. S.F.: Short for "staple fiber," a textile developed in the early twentieth century as a substitute for cotton.

Blushing like a virgin, Mother did not go on.

(You see, my foreign friends, at Japanese hot springs, the sexes often bathe together, using only a towel as a means of covering up.)

"Who cares?" I said sarcastically. "That's the new moral of the Japanese aggressor."

"Ah!" my father seethed. "So you've given even your soul to those damn Chinese!"

3. The Tragedy of the Mailbox

Steel! Steel! Steel!

All of Japan is crazy for steel.

. . .

One day my brother wrote to us from the Central China front. In his letter we read: "Recently, every letter that we get from Japan is wet beyond legibility. Does the government care so little about transporting things for the army?"

I wrote him back:

Dear brother, in your homeland, people have nothing to give other than their tears. While these are becoming cheaper every day, every other thing is becoming terribly expensive. Casting their gaze hopelessly westward, wives weep, children weep, mothers weep, and female mail-carriers, a new sight on our streets, weep for husbands, fathers, and brothers never to return again. Even the mailbox weeps. Ah, do you know, dear brother, that in Japan there are more than one hundred thousand mailboxes, of which twenty thousand are made from steel. One month ago, these steel boxes were swapped out with substitutes that are so delicate that if it rains, they all burst into tears, making our already wet letters even wetter. So dearest brother, remember: in Japan, twenty thousand mailboxes are weeping, and in China those old twenty thousand,

An Age of Substitutes—Vignettes of Wartime Japan   147

now in the form of bullets, are making your innocent neighbors weep....

4. Replacement Men

The House of Representatives...

How peacefully the ministers convene during the war! The air itself seems laced with narcotics. The national mobilization has silenced not only the people but also their garrulous representatives. No questions, no debate. The representatives sleep. Some even smack their foreheads against their desks. Security guards armed with mints and brushes go back and forth among them, trying to wake them up. "Hear, hear," they mutter comically in their half-sleep. Meanwhile, without obstacle, the military budget passes—an unprecedented sum of six billion.

To my left, a middle-aged man, seemingly from the country, murmurs angrily. "What an idiot! That Yamada fellow promised to increase the subsidy to our village, so I voted for him. But the devil, he hasn't said even a single word about it since the election. Ah, why didn't I vote for Yamano, who I hear gave three yen to everyone who voted for him!"

To my right, two modern girls are talking sleepily.[3]

"All those representatives do is say 'Hear, hear.'"

"I know! It would be better if we elected parrots. With a little practice, those birds would be able to say 'Hear, hear' better and more beautifully than these local representatives with their incomprehensible rural accents."

The Speaker of the House rises.

"The budget has passed by unanimous consent. This is cause for celebration! Now, I have one final proposal to add. Please listen. Ahem—the war has produced a labor shortage everywhere, but here we have more men than is necessary. That is why

---

3. Modern girls (*moga*): A Japanese term used to refer to young urban women with a marked interest in Westernized fashion.

you, my good representatives, also must go to the front, fields, and factories. This way you can be truly loyal children of His Imperial Majesty. However, according to the constitution, the Parliament cannot hold sessions without a majority of its members in attendance. So let it be decided that the next time we are to meet you will be replaced with puppets." And slapping the table, he exclaims: "Agreed?"

Not knowing what is going on, the startled representatives in the front sputter out as usual, "Hear, hear!," while those in the back go right on napping.

A ringing bell announces the closing of the session.

There is noise all around.

Was I also sleeping along with the representatives? But wait—?! Ah, this is my room.

I rub my eyes vigorously.

On the table, I see a Japanese newspaper. Outside I can hear automobiles and people running about. I have been woken by an air strike alarm—it was not the bell of the Japanese House of Representatives after all.

August 1939, Chongqing

12

WOMEN WORKERS IN WARTIME JAPAN

THE FASCISTS ARE WELL AWARE THAT the emancipation of women from the home will render them no profit. But because of the war, which they themselves started to satisfy their grand ambitions and selfish desires, they have had to inadvertently retract even their beloved slogan of "Women to the kitchen!" What this ideological self-contradiction will ultimately result in, they, at present, cannot afford to care. And so, a great many women have begun to appear in all manner of working environments.

But before we get to that, let us take a brief look at the country, which has become a firm pillar of support for the current invasion.

In the country, women have long played an important role in production, a role that has only grown since the outbreak of the war, as the majority of soldiers fighting in the Japanese army are supplied by the villages. Furthermore, because of an "uneven munitions prosperity," many men have left for the city. Horses and cows have been requisitioned, and owing to the national steel shortage, agricultural tools have not only become more costly but are often wholly unavailable for purchase. The same can be said for fertilizer, which has had to be rationed, as the majority must be imported from overseas. To cover for such shortages and, to an extent, maintain production in the rural areas, the state has had to mobilize the women. In fact, according to data compiled by the Ministry of Agriculture and Forestry, during the peak farming season of last spring the average ratio of male and female workers in landed farming on a national level was 46.0:48.1 [*sic*]. Therefore, it may be said that Japan's agricultural industry now depends largely on women.

However, women's advancement in the country is chiefly characterized by a redistribution and intensification of labor caused by a reduced male population. Seen in this light, the absolute number of women employed in production has, in fact, fallen. We must not forget that, even before the war, farmers' expenses generally exceeded their incomes, and now, thanks to direct and indirect influences of the war menacing from every side, many of our farmers do not have even one grain of rice to eat three months after the autumn harvest. Debts mount until their last piece of land has bid them farewell. Of course, such a state is especially acute among the families of soldiers at the front. Wives and daughters of poor and middle-class tenant farmers are increasingly leaving for the city to work as domestics, cooks, and prostitutes, among other occupations. Factory doors in particular stand wide open and ready to absorb them. Last December, the magazine *Kakushin* dispatched Kusumoto Yukiko as a special correspondent to Southern Japan, where she reported that in several villages there is not even one young man or woman to be found.

Now then, let us turn to the cities.

What change has occurred there?

The streets of Tokyo and Osaka have lately been beautified with women police officers and mail carriers. Certainly, this is one of the new wartime sights. Wherever you go, you seem to meet freshly minted women workers.

But even more worthy of note is the "rapid progress" that women have made in industry—especially heavy industry.

The mobilization of women for heavy labor is called "the women's front." The last world war organized an astounding number of European women in an industrial army hitherto rarely seen on the factory floors of the machine and metal industries. Now the same phenomenon is occurring in Japan, where the number of women working in home-front manufacturing has increased to a startling degree.

Here are some figures published by the Factory Section of the Tokyo Metropolitan Police Department concerning every factory employing more than fifty women in Tokyo:

June 1937 (Just before the war)	100 women
December 1938	135 women
(Men: 168)	
Only at machine works:	196 women
(Men: 189)	

Another national survey shows:

March 1937	100 women
March 1938	
Light industry:	101 women
(Men: 107)	
Heavy industry:	151 women
(Men: 137)	

Can we reason that greater employment for women in home-front production is simply owing to a lack of men, or to women's social progress? Time was when the capitalist owners of silk factories and spinning mills ignored the great industrial reserve army of men, choosing to exclusively employ women. Were they feminists? Don't make me laugh! Those vampires were merely drawn to the low wages, obedience, and disorganization that have become second nature to women after being bound to the kitchen for thousands of years. Nothing has changed, even today. Furthermore, the women of wartime Japan are, as you surely know, temporarily or permanently deprived of husbands and brothers, which only compounds the burden of endless inflation. To buy bread for themselves and their family, they would jump into the fire if need be. And yet, if soldiers returning from the front were to demand their former employment back, these women would likely be dismissed with but one word, sent packing into streets of scarcity to silently accept their fate.

> "The Women's Front Is Flourishing!"
> "A Boom in Female Employment Agencies!"
> "Men Pale at Good Pay for Women Workers!"

These are nothing more than empty headlines that decorate the fronts of newspapers and magazines. Time after time, they betray their beautiful sentiments, baring the misery below the surface. Let us now acquaint ourselves with the lives of women workers using data provided by such "exposés."

We will start by getting a clear picture of wages in numbers.[1]

Riken Machine Works, Takasaki[2]
    Starting wage: 55 sen/day (plus travel expenses and summer and winter work clothes)

A munitions factory in Itabashi, Tokyo
    Starting wage: Less than 70 sen/day

Nakajima Aircraft Plant
    Starting wage: 60 sen/day

Riken Machine Works, Kashiwazaki
    Starting wage: 30–40 sen/day

---

1. Author's note: 100 sen = 1 yen.

2. Author's note: This factory may be considered a model for most factories in Japan, where the number of male and female workers is the same and

Note that the average daily wage nationwide for women spinners, whose industry has long been famous for its terrible exploitation, is 70.2 sen.

Now let us compare the women with their male counterparts.

Tokyo Electric Company
    Starting wage:

Women:	85 sen/day
Men:	160 sen/day

A fountain-pen factory in Osaka
    Starting wage:

Women:	1,500 sen/month
Men:	1,700 sen/month

A printer in Tachikawa
    Apprentice wage:

Women:	40 sen/day
Men:	60 sen/day

A dry battery factory in Osaka
    Starting wage:

Women:	65–130 sen/day
Men:	110–230 sen/day

There is also a gap in the postwar average rate of nominal wage increases (i.e., excluding wages earned from night work, etc.) among men and women working in heavy industry. From March 1937 to March 1938, that of women has been 2.9 percent, while that of men has been 3.4 percent. Still more remarkable to learn is that women's wages have risen more slowly and more incrementally than those of men. For example, at Kamata Electric Works, the starting wage for women is 75 sen a day and in general

---

where 80 percent of the women have finished the highest level of secondary school, while 20 percent have finished the highest level of primary school.

reaches 80 sen after two or three years. The highest wage given to a veteran woman worker is only 130 sen, while that of a man employed to do the very same job is 320 sen.

As we have just seen, the wage ratio for worker men and women is:

Maximum:	2:1
Minimum:	6:5
Average:	3:2

So do women work less hard than men? No, no—not even in heavy industry—no! As the Factory Section of the Tokyo Metropolitan Police has observed: "At machine works, women are not inferior to their male counterparts."

At Riken Machine Works, Takasaki, the number of male and female workers is the same—that is, 350 persons each, but, as a spokesperson for the factory has noted, women could occupy 90 percent of the workforce if need be. A dry battery factory in Osaka employs 120 women and 80 men. And an unidentified machine works has asserted that it is not necessary to mobilize all of its working men. In fact, Toyoda Automatic Works, in Aichi, runs exclusively on female labor. Accordingly, the sphere of female labor has grown to include everything from inspectors, recorders, fitters, and adjusters to turners and polishers. Regarding lathe work, the same work performed by men and women results in the same number of bad products. The ratio of output on the lathe, which requires sensitivity, precision, and endurance, is 1.25:1 for women and men. Tanaka Shōichi of Riken Heavy Industries has boasted: "Let us assume that a skilled worker (employed at 200 sen/day) can do 50 units per day. If we make him do 60 units, he will become physically and mentally exhausted. But we have taught the same job to an ignorant girl (employed at 50 sen/day) and have ordered her to be hard-working and diligent. Now she can do 100 units per day."

Behold the exploitation!

Fascist agents tout the rapid growth in wages among women workers. This is not a total lie. At several factories wages have risen by 10–15 percent since the outbreak of war (which is still less than what the men earn). But the increases are only nominal. First, we must consider the skyrocketing inflation. As of May 1, the average retail price index for daily necessities showed an increase of 1.5 percent over one month and 1.7 percent over one year. According to a survey by the Cabinet Statistics Bureau, before the war the cost-of-living index for workers nationwide was growing at a rate of less than 4 percent per year but from July 1937 (the start of the war) to July 1938, by 12 percent! Meanwhile, as we all know, the wages of working women do not grow proportional to inflation.

Second, we must consider the changing role of women in the family system. Previously, most women played a supportive role for their husbands, fathers, and brothers. Now, instead of supporting those taken away by the war, they must support the whole family themselves. Even men, who earn more than women thanks to higher wages, regular employment, and long night shifts, complain of a general difficulty in getting by. According to a study by *Keihin Industrial Magazine,* a model worker with a daily wage of 200 sen, with a family of seven, who neither smokes nor drinks, earns a net income of 8,016 sen, spends 8,740 sen per month, and barely covers the deficit with his semi-annual bonus. If this be true, the misery of a woman worker with a family must be beyond words!

This brings us to another matter: working hours and factory facilities. The following are the bare minimum required by women workers:

1. Proper hygienic facilities for women employed at the factory
2. A working day that does not cause chronic exhaustion
3. A minimum wage that can support a healthy diet
4. A day care, nursing room, and paid leave for illnesses and pre-/postnatal maternity

Ah, but wartime Japan "does not have time" for such things! And so, women must work at least ten, but more often fourteen to eighteen hours, a day in diabolically indecent conditions, either to make up for labor shortages or to supplement their meagre incomes. Moreover, women workers are not men, who enjoy complete freedom as soon as they step outside of the factory gate. Straight home the women must go, where the cooking, cleaning, and childcare await them. On top of this, they are expected to build care packages, sew war amulets, and make every arrangement for soldiers shipping out or returning home. The tasks weigh heavily upon their already burdened shoulders.

The mere thought of having an accident or falling ill is enough to make any woman worker tremble. Statistics speak volumes about the sudden increase in injuries among women in machine and instrument plants:

April 1937	852 accidents
August 1937	1,283 accidents

The ratio of women absent from illness is in fact greater than that of men. The following numbers are for the second half of 1938:

Women:	12–19.9
Men:	11–18.5

As to beriberi and lung diseases—or "factory illnesses"— we have no exact numbers, as there has not been enough time to collect data. Yet every factory doctor attests to a great rise in the number of patients with such afflictions.

Last, I must draw your attention to the destruction of motherhood wrought by the cruel and unusual expansion of the "women's front." Indeed, there has been a sudden growth in abnormal pregnancies, infant mortality, juvenile delinquency, immorality, and even physical deterioration among young people, which, after twenty years, is now confronting the European nations that had taken part in the last world war.

A Tokyo municipal survey has observed a notable increase in stillbirths for this year. Regarding juvenile delinquents, the Tokyo Juvenile Court dealt with 10,165 cases of delinquency in 1937 and almost 11,200 cases as of October 1938. In December, protection offices (ancillaries of the Juvenile Court) were established in Tokyo, Osaka, and Nagoya.

Having suffered all manner of oppression and exploitation doubly—as women suffering under entrenched feudalism and as proletarians suffering under capitalism—Japanese women workers were already among "the most miserable creatures" in the world. Now a more than two-year-old "holy war" foists "the duty of a loyal citizen" upon them, who in ordinary times do not enjoy a single right or protection of citizenship.

How long can women workers be expected to put up with such endless oppression, exploitation, exhaustion, and hunger?

In some respects, their "obedience" is truly something to behold. And yet it is not in the nature of Japanese women to be obedient, as the bourgeoisie will have us believe. Their obedience was formed by the long history and traditions of their society. And as long as they are bound to the kitchen, the "logic" of the bourgeoisie will appear to hold water. But if you take them out of the home, throw them into the workplace, and give them a collective life and social role, their "obedience" (which is what the capitalists are so happy to hire them for) will inevitably change and come undone. The facts do not lie. Just look at the women workers employed at silk factories and spinning mills. Before anyone expected, they have learned how to organize and fight and on several occasions have forced and won strikes to raise wages and improve workplace conditions. Municipal bus companies in Tokyo began hiring women as conductors because they could pay them low wages, use them in place of "rebellious" male workers, and by any means sow conflict among the sexes—that is, they wished to "kill two birds with one stone." However, the women foiled this foul plot and, together with the men, are now fighting against a common enemy. Indeed, their name has long been hailed as the most class-conscious group among women workers in Japan.

Wartime Japan's brutal censorship makes every effort to shield the public from antifascist or antiwar activity. And yet we know that women from poor villages in Yamagata and Aomori, workers' wives, and women workers in Senju, Kawasaki, and Osaka have shed much blood for the "collective rescue" of family members sent off to war.

Even those worker women who, after the outbreak of war, volunteered to make care packages and sew war amulets now refuse to do so unless forced to from above. Only female fascists who feed on chauvinism continue without complaint or derision. Recall that women workers were once active participants in the proletarian movement, though they lacked a historical foundation. Now they are making use of their valuable experience and in manufacturing have grown in both quantity and quality. Therefore, let no one assume a retreat or a recess in their struggle.

Japan's rulers are eager to promote a drop in strike activity as proof of "the nation's unanimous support for the holy war," a conflict they themselves have falsely invented. But even this is unmasked, whether consciously or not, by the newspapers and magazines supposedly under their control. A mouse driven into a corner will bite even a cat. Strikes, which have actually increased over the last year, are mostly concerned with the pressing needs of "higher wages," "shorter working days," and "the installation of factory facilities for the welfare of all workers." While a law limiting the factory working day was implemented last May, without the "goodwill" of employers, this law amounts to nothing more than a wage cut. Therefore, here and there workers are using sabotage, demanding fourteen-and-a-half hours' payment for every twelve hours of work.

Now a new form of sabotage has emerged: intentionally

making defective helmets, tanks, and other war goods. Forging iron to create such goods is hard work. So the workers' weary bodies and disdain for the ongoing war have given birth to many bullet-vulnerable helmets and tanks. The frequent fires at munitions factories across the nation, too, cannot be seen as purely accidental and caused by workers' fatigue.

These strikes, sabotages, antiwar actions, and other struggles that are undoubtedly taking place, though not widely known, are being carried out by men and women cooperatively. Women workers, who are now actively taking part in social production alongside the men, have learned from the hardship of real life that their profit is in no way unique to women but is inseparable from that of all workers. They have at last realized that the union is their one and only tool of resistance, for it is the union that terrifies their enemies the most. Indeed, many factory owners avoid even setting up a "Group for Industrial Patriotic Service" under the Ministry for Health because, in their experience, giving workers any opportunity to organize is sure to be the mother of misfortune!

Having suffered the painful effects of war the hardest, in the most real and profound way, women workers will naturally become the strongest antiwar vanguard on the home front. They will organize, form a united front with the men, and mobilize their sisters in the countryside, other workplaces, and at home. Moreover, they will work with soldiers at the front—and together they will bring about an all-out battle against the militarists. If you find this to be an overestimation of their abilities, I ask you to look to Russia in 1905 and 1917. Who do you think it was that stood up, at the risk of their lives, to call for "bread and peace"? Were those women workers under czarism not just like our Japanese women and proletarians, oppressed, exploited, and drowning in despair because of imperialist wars (first between Russia and Japan and now worldwide)? To borrow the words of Lenin: "Without them [the women] we should not have been victorious."

I believe that as the invasion continues, the revolutionary struggle of women workers will grow stronger and wider. At the same time, I sincerely hope that it will succeed as soon as possible. For they are my sisters in blood.

September 1939

13

A PROFILE OF JAPANESE STUDENTS

IN THE BUDGET OF THE MINISTRY OF EDUCATION, there used to be a "fund for thought rectification," a rather significant sum earmarked for high schools and universities. This was during the early 1930s. Now, I don't know what was done with this money at other schools, but at our school, aside from being used to invite some or other famous anti-Marxist professor to give lectures, most of the money—presuming the administrators were at a loss as how to use it—was spent on sweets for clubs and class picnics.

At the time, the reactionists had begun their iron-fisted rule, and the fear of Bolshevization among the student body was beginning to subside, so the next generation would surely not have the honor of enjoying these sweets. Nevertheless, the traditional policy of promoting sports and games instead of rigorous study continued long after, and without dispute. Indeed, it was in this way that the government succeeded in indoctrinating many impressionable students, who came to see baseball as a way of student life and find in school an extension of the dance hall, coffee house, or other such entertainment venue.

A friend who runs a pawnshop once told me:

"Students come to me to pawn their school books; in summer, winter clothes; and in winter, summer clothes. They sometimes even try to pawn their IDs! Heaven only knows what they need the money for, though some quite shamelessly explain to me that one night in Tamanoi costs them upwards of two yen."[1]

That said, they diligently take notes during compulsory lectures and will even pull a few all-nighters at the end of each term, for they clearly understand that in such a society as theirs, and in such a stagnant economy as that which they have inherited from their elders, if they do not have influential friends or relations, only a good test score can guarantee a good future for them. Politics they avoid at all costs.

I can cite many examples but shall limit myself to just one:

After the February 26 Incident (an attempted fascist coup that took place in 1936), I asked my cousin, who was then studying at Tokyo Imperial University, what the students there had to say about it.

"Nothing," the dear man-child said stoically. "But they're starting to worry it could result in exams being postponed."

Of course, not every student is of this sort. Still, it must be admitted that such an attitude is typical of students today. Here and there one may hear voices of discontent and censure regarding the unprecedented chaos and heresy in education. And yet there is nobody and nothing that can help to remedy the situation.

It was in this state that the war of aggression broke out. What change has it caused for the students? To start, there has been a strong rebuke of their hedonistic lifestyle. And on several occasions, the morality squad have conducted mass arrests of those "indecent" citizens at every place of amusement under the sun.

On this topic, allow me to cite the testimony of one police officer:

"Sitting before me, with his head lowered, was K., a student of Waseda University. Although I tried to explain to him the

---

1. Tamanoi: An infamous red-light district in Tokyo, situated on the east bank of the Sumida River.

significance of the war, the national situation, and the duty of students, I could sense that I was only wasting my breath. Everything—indeed, *everything*—he already knew much better than I did myself! At last he opened his mouth and expressed how he found his lessons dull, and his dormitory boring: 'So why must I be forbidden from looking for distractions elsewhere?' 'But tell me,' I implored, 'have you given no thought to your peers at the front?' To which he responded, 'When I receive the order to go to war, I too will drop everything and go, butcher the enemy, and willingly kill myself if need be.' At this, the youth flashed a vacant smile. Oh, what a vacant smile! Even my hardened policeman's heart felt the prick of its sting."

In the end, the policeman concluded:

"Most of the students I have dealt with more or less share this attitude."

Such facts cannot but cause grief to our educational authorities. In the spring and summer of last year, Spiritualist-General Araki Sadao, then minister of education, called for a series of educational reforms and improvements, culminating in the creation of a theory (?!) that he called an "Education for Asian Prosperity." Now, it is not hard to see that, like his famous moustache, General Araki's "theory" may look grand but is in fact devoid of substance. It is the by-product of the "New Order in East Asia," and it is to this that it owes its character as an educational "theory." But however eloquently the fascists may choose to phrase it, their "New Order" is nothing more than a policy for establishing the absolute hegemony of the Japanese Empire over East Asia, effected by the suppression of all other nations in the region and the expulsion of European interests. General Araki has emphasized two aims in his "Education for Asian Prosperity":

1. To give students an ardent spirit of public service.
2. To give them a full knowledge of the continent.

Which means, in other words:

164   On Fascist Japan

1. To teach them to support the invasion.
2. To teach them to rule the continent.

To accomplish the first aim, the state has sought to:

a. Increase military drills in schools.
b. Enforce labor service.
c. Shorten the delay of the student draft.

Of (a) and (c), I imagine one needs no further explanation. As for (b), the enforcement of labor service, this has various purposes, one of which is to supplement the national labor shortage. Last April, the government introduced collective labor as a regular course at coed middle schools and high schools. This so-called course consists of construction work in cities and villages, assistance to families of mobilized soldiers, agricultural work, and general public service. Moreover, this May, the vice ministers of education and agriculture and forestry directed the prefectural governors to enlist the most able students to plough fields, sow seeds, transplant crops, weed grass, control pests, take in the harvest, and cultivate silkworms. Indeed, in some prefectures students were apparently worked so hard that they barely had time to attend their other classes.

To make us "good citizens," the state once spoiled us with sweets. Now they want us to sweat and form hard calluses.

My, how the times have changed!

Labor service is often characterized by a strange formality. In some places, absolute silence is required; elsewhere you may be ordered to recite a part of the national origin myth. And fluttering above at all times are imperial flags, like overseers, threatening to condemn the lazy as "unpatriotic."

This course of enslavement has resulted in several farces. At some schools in Tokyo, where there is no suitable labor service available, students are ordered to dig holes in the corners of the schoolyard and then fill them in again. Among the expenses listed for labor service at one university were 230 yen for sweets. After all, a gentleman cannot be expected to carry a heavy load without the promise of a reward! Last year, and the year before that, summer vacation was abolished because of the labor-service system. Taking advantage of this, some private schools had students, instead of hiring workers, carry out landfill work for the construction of a new wing and saved a sufficient sum of money. More cunning school administrators tried to collect tuition fees for August under the pretense that such a nominal holiday costs the school a lot of money.

But I fear we have now dwelled far too long upon this subject. So let us hasten on to the second aim of General Araki's so-called theory.

Last spring, looking to teach students how to one day rule the continent, the Ministry of Education organized a student brigade of five hundred members, operating on a budget of 80,000 yen, which it employed to carry out cultural, pacification, and engineering missions in Manchuria and North China for one month in the summer. Should this prove successful, the scale of the pilot project will be expanded.

And so students are, on the one hand, pulled like livestock by the national policy while, on the other hand, criticized for not being studious. But according to the students themselves: "Once we finish our schooling, the government will force us to join the army. And to a mere soldier, all culture, all intellect, all science is superfluous—a hindrance even."

Indeed, the war has driven healthy people to the slaughterhouse, useless intellectuals to unemployment (according to a study conducted by the *Miyako shinbun*, in December 1938, 340 graduates from the Department of Literature at Tokyo Imperial University were looking for work, but only seven workplaces had posted job offers), and much-needed engineers to despair. (It is unfortunate, says Professor Yamanouchi of the Department of Mechanical Engineering at Tokyo Imperial University, but even if a student would like a job in spinning or some other peacetime industry, the government will force him to accept work in a munitions plant.)

What can be done? War is war!

"What can be done?" "Nothing will help!" For the past seven years or so, such exclamations have become the stance of a vast majority of students toward everything. Writhing in its death throes, capitalism offers them no hope for a life beyond graduation, while fascism has taken away every right and freedom owed to them as individuals, as national citizens. They have lost what was good in the self and have gained what is bad from the collective. Most of them know that the invasion is wrong. And yet they lack the courage to actively resist it.

There are still too few fighting against the war.

I am reminded of something written by Mushanokōji Saneatsu a few months ago:

"My daughter was asked by one of her classmates: 'Why doesn't your father protest the war like he did before?' To which my daughter responded: 'Because such a protest would do no good now.' 'But,' her friend pressed on, 'when people like your father keep silent, it disheartens us, for we are waiting for them to speak up.'"[2]

Behold, the weakness of our intelligentsia!

However—and here allow me to paraphrase the words of another famous writer—saying such things will only make our students laugh. They will tell you that such melancholy belongs to the nineteenth century. Perhaps they are right. But to which century belongs the premature apathy behind such expressions as "It's not our problem"? Is that not also reached by way of melancholy under a system of absolute oppression?

Students! Why, they ought to be a symbol of flowering

---

2. Mushanokōji Saneatsu (1885–1976): A writer who, during World War I, became celebrated as an antiwar humanist. His disappearance from the literary world during the rise of fascism in Japan was likely encouraged by his older brother, Kintomo, who was an ambassador to Nazi Germany.

youth. But a merciless storm of fascism will not allow them to fully bloom. And so, in order to survive their current environment, unbeknownst to themselves, they have had to learn the art of self-preservation.

"One night," writes Hirotsu Kazuo in *Chuō kōron* (Central Review),

> while chatting with friends, we reached the conclusion that, should the war continue long enough, there could potentially come a day when the proportion of men to women in Japan is 1:15.[3] "Hah!" responded a middle-aged man with his head bowed low in dismay. "What a shame! If that should come to pass, each of us would have to feed fifteen women when one wife is quite the burden already." Then a student next to me chimed in with a laugh: "Well, I have a completely different view of the matter. I would receive 10 yen a month from each woman. That's 150 yen! Why, it's better than being employed by a company."

Naturally, this remark was likely only said in jest. And yet I believe it throws into stark relief for us a profile of students today in Fascist Japan.

January 1940, Chongqing

---

3. Hirotsu Kazuo (1891–1968): A novelist and critic. In the 1930s he grew attracted to the proletarian literature movement, though his allegiance was ultimately to the Japanese Empire, which he supported in its colonization efforts in China and Korea.

14

JAPAN AT A CROSSROADS

WITH EACH PASSING DAY, I am growing increasingly eager to hear from the people of my homeland, which I left eight years ago. However, I have yet to hear anything. What I have heard from the Three Islands are indeed Japanese voices, but not those of my comrades.[1] To be sure, the choice of words used by these other Japanese voices is new, but still, I cannot trust them. I have always hated them and will continue to do so.

I do not know what the Allies saw in the impassive Japanese upon arriving on their shores. Perhaps they already knew the true nature of this "belligerent" race. For the past eight years, the Japanese have quietly shed rivers, if not oceans, of blood, sweat, and tears. But you reap what you sow. And the Japanese will have to atone for their sins.

Atonement is necessary. That said, I am firmly opposed to "punishment," for that will only spur this belligerent nation to another war.

I am not being funny. I am speaking the cold, hard truth

---

1. Three Islands: Given that the "other Japanese voices" are those of Japan's political and military elite, Hasegawa is probably referring to Japan as a whole, even though the archipelago is typically considered to comprise four or five main islands (i.e., Hokkaidō, Honshū, Shikoku, Kyūshū, and Okinawa).

and honestly fear that my beloved homeland may become a hotbed for World War III. That is the root of my sincere opposition, and I am not alone in it, for surely the Japanese people as a whole oppose it also, along with all the people of the world.

Who can say that we have not shed enough bitter tears; that mankind only exists for destruction, reprisals, and annihilation; that peace and happiness are unattainable and nothing more than a beautiful dream?

We must root out fascism, the sworn enemy of mankind.

In the West, Nazi criminals have for the most part been arrested or have had to flee to the ends of the earth. But in the East, Japanese fascists are still freely breathing the same air as us. What's more, they are conveniently discarding their old warrior garb and donning the costumes of peace and democracy.

We were victorious. But do not make the mistake of thinking that Japan's surrender has somehow ushered in a new era of peace.

The surrender was not owing to the fact that its military strength was exhausted or that it felt compassion for its people. It witnessed the fate of the Nazis. The Potsdam Declaration called on Japan to "follow the path of reason." And it was reason that caused it to surrender. After all, it did not want to be annihilated.

Put simply, Japan's swift surrender came about because its ruling elite wanted to preserve as much of its power as possible.

Some critics may be disappointed by the lack of regret currently being expressed by the Shōwa emperor, Suzuki [Kantarō] and Higashikuni [Naruhiko].[2] Indeed, this is no more evident than in the anger that they feel toward the selection of the new cabinet. But what are these critics really expecting of the Japanese aggressors? Do they still not realize that these men are the same old

---

2. The Shōwa emperor: Emperor Hirohito (1901–1989). Suzuki Kantarō (1868–1948): An admiral in the Imperial Japanese Navy and prime minister of Japan from April 7 to August 17, 1945. Higashikuni Naruhiko (1887–1990): A Japanese imperial prince, military officer, and prime minister of Japan from August 17 to October 9, 1945.

fascists and manufacturers of war? Once the Allies have begun their Occupation in earnest, the old guard will likely pretend to be peaceful and democratic. Its members will surely claim that, even as they crushed their political opponents, "they did it all for France"; that they had given their lives to their country.

Others mistakenly think that by settling the scores of Pearl Harbor and Bataan there will be peace in the world. They hope that moderates, business clans, nobles, and bureaucrats will govern the future Japan.

How terribly wrong they are!

What difference, if any, is there between so-called moderates and extremists? Within the context of a fascist state whose army is employed in invading other nations, it is nothing more than a matter of intensity. Today, having given some careful consideration to the present world order, Japan's moderates are only acting moderate out of respect for the military might of the US and Britain. As for the imperialist-capitalists, they are now starving the masses to develop foreign markets. If the military clans were the outriders of the invasion, the business clans were its driving force, all while politicians threatened the people with bayonets and laws. Each of these groups contributed to the invasion in no small way. In effect, they are each one-third of an authoritarian apparatus.

To the Chinese people, I say that Japan's fascists have still not admitted to defeat in the Sino-Japanese War. Consider how the emperor's August 15 address and the Suzuki Cabinet Declaration only refer to the Great East Asian War of the past "four" years while remaining silent on the blood debts owed to China over the past eight years. What's more, they are playing the trump cards of "collaboration" and "friendship." Surely, the Chinese people cannot allow them to sugarcoat the bloody truth.

We must uncover this foul plot. We must break it wide open. The peace we demand is not provisional but everlasting.

We are not asking for a Japan built on anti-Bolshevism. We want a democratic Japan!

We must abolish Japanese fascism—its chief agents, systems, military, economy, and thought must be utterly uprooted!

"Let the Japanese people decide for themselves whether they should have an emperor"—this is all well and good, but the imperial dictatorship still exists. Are the Japanese people really free, then, to do away with the emperor when the governing structure that places him at its center has not changed?

Arms manufacturing may be prohibited and peacetime industries restored, but so long as the state belongs to the old elite, all peacetime industries can pivot to wartime industries on a dime—in the name of "national prosperity."

Uprooting Japanese fascism and building a democratic Japan will be an impossible task if we merely rely on the military strength of the Allied forces while looking down on the democratic capacity of the Japanese people.

Years ago, many people—especially in China—supported the revolutionary movement in Japan. At the time, the full-scale invasion of China was only two years in, and there was a hope that the Japanese people would rally against war and bring it to a swift end. But things did not turn out so. Now the Japanese are denounced as fanatical adherents of fascism, or at least as pitiful and foolish sheep.

I admit that the poison of fascism has seeped deep into the Japanese populace at large. But even under wartime oppression, acts of sabotage and strikes broke out at munitions plants across the country, while the nation's jails swelled with men and women accused of thought crimes and treason. These two facts alone prove to me that Japan's revolutionary movement did not decline during the war.

The Allies may be disappointed to find that many Japanese people do not consider their wartime dissidents to be liberators. However, this should come as no surprise. Let us not forget that since the outbreak of the Great Pacific War, Japan's rulers have decried the "ruin of the nation" and the "downfall of the people" in an effort to threaten and deceive its own people.

"Defeat" and "colonization"—what terrible words these are for the Japanese! After all, they witnessed the tragedies in Taiwan and Korea themselves. Their rulers had called Manchuria the "promised land," even though no Japanese person in their right mind believed such nonsense. It is perhaps for this very reason that the Japanese cannot help but eye with suspicion that paragraph in the Potsdam Declaration that begins "We do not intend that the Japanese shall be enslaved as a race or destroyed as a nation."

Among those who for years had their eyes covered and ears plugged, there are probably many who believe that Japan's defeat was merely due to the Soviet invasion and the use of atomic weapons. Such critics do not yet realize that the victory for the Allies was a victory for democracy everywhere. Indeed, for the Japanese people the significance of the Allied forces on their shores is not yet fully understood.

So is Japan's ruling elite working to bring about this understanding?

Absolutely not!

It is intervening between the Allies and the people. It is still scheming to cover the eyes, plug the ears, and close the mouths of the people.

And so, for every day that the ruling elite continue to wield power, the Japanese people will be another day behind. Higashikuni has claimed that the Japanese constitution gives its people the freedoms of speech, assembly, press, and religion. But again, if the ruling elite can still arrest and torture the people at will, are the people really free? I ask you this: Is the elite presently fostering the rise of a popular democratic revolution? Will it immediately release all of its political prisoners, excepting those guilty of fascism? Will it allow Japanese revolutionary groups in China, including Okano Susumu's Liberation League, to return to their native soil and resume their activities?[3]

---

3. Okano Susumu: Hasegawa is referring to the wartime alias of Sanzō Nosaka (1892–1993), one of the founders of the Japanese Communist Party.

The Potsdam Declaration states: "There must be eliminated for all time the authority and influence of those who have deceived and misled the people of Japan into embarking on world conquest." Indeed, this authority and influence must be eliminated for all time. But if so, this must be carried out promptly and thoroughly.

Although Japan has already made its formal surrender in writing, the Allied forces have been surprisingly slow to disarm its army in the Occupied territories and elsewhere. Do not be fooled. Disarmament will take more than a few days. The Japanese ruling class is determined to prolong its life and retain its power.

For this reason, we fervently hope that the attitude of the Allied forces toward the ruling class is temporary and transitional.

However, we must not lose a moment. The fat hands that the Japanese elite are offering to the Allies are wicked and evil hands that have killed and been washed of blood. Behind their deceitful smiles, there lurks a terrible plot.

Do not forget that the chief agents, structures, and economy of Japanese fascism, as well as its military might, continue to exist unchecked.

We hope and pray that all those who are guilty of war crimes will be arrested without delay and that a standard will be applied both broadly and thoroughly. Okano Susumu's "Punishment for War Criminals," a section of his pamphlet *The Path to Eliminating Japanese Fascism,* will serve as a good reference.[4] Human garbage like Sano [Manabu] and Nabeyama [Sadachika], who were once members of the Japanese Communist Party but later collaborated with the fascists in Northern and Central China, should also be included among the war criminals. When making arrests, the people of both Japan and China should work together with the Allies to pursue the guilty parties to the ends of the earth,

---

4. *The Path to Eliminating Japanese Fascism:* Hasegawa is referring to the title of the Chinese edition (*Xiaomie riben faxisi de daolu*) of Susumu/Sanzō's *Building a Democratic Japan.* For the original, see Sanzō Nosaka, *Minshuteki nihon no kensetsu* (Kiryū, Japan: Akatsuki shobō, 1947).

174 On Fascist Japan

if need be. Let us, to this end, fully and immediately eliminate the chief agents, apparatuses, economy, military might, and thought of the ruling class.

Let us wipe out, once and for all, from the face of the earth, Japanese fascism, which is the enemy of all mankind.

Let us have eternal peace!

Let us have a democratic Japan!

Having been abroad for eight years, there is nothing that I miss more than my home. My only hope is that it will not revert to the erupting volcano it once was but will remain always a beautiful island on the Pacific.

September 7, 1945

Further Readings

Original Uncollected Works by Hasegawa Teru

Anonymous. "Amikiĝa kunveno kun nacilingvaj literaturistoj." *Majo*, no. 2 (July 1936).

Anonymous. "Ĉindon-ja." *Infanoj sur tutmondo*, no. 6 (1936).

Anonymous. "Japana lingvo." *Infanoj sur tutmondo*, no. 6 (1936).

Anonymous. "Kiel oni nomas Esperante japanajn infanojn." *Infanoj sur tutmondo*, no. 6 (1936).

Anonymous. "'Kroniko de eŭropa scienco' Surscenigita." *Majo*, no. 2 (July 1936).

Anonymous. "Saluton!" *Infanoj sur tutmondo*, no. 6 (1936).

Dull Fool. "Nukarumi." *Kōyū*, no. 9 (July 1932).

Hasegawa Teru. "Banshun shoka shō." *Kōyū*, no. 8 (July 1931).

———. "Historieto de japana literature." *La revuo orienta* (February 1935).

———. "Katasumi no aki." *Kōyū*, no. 8 (July 1931).

———. "Printempa frenezo." *Esperanto bungaku* (May–June 1934).

———. "Ses Monatoj." *Esperanto bungaku* (November–December 1934).

Luchuan Yingzi. "Zài qílù shàng de rìběn." *Xinhua ribao*, September 11, 1945.

Scienculo. "Kiel formiĝis Monto Huĵi." *Infanoj sur tutmondo*, no. 6 (1936).

Verda Majo. "Esperante aŭ nacilingve?" *Esperanto bungaku* (October 1935).

———. "Esperanto kaj demokratio." *Lernilo de Esperanto* (November–December 1943).

176 Further Readings

———. "Kiel lerni?" *Lernilo de Esperanto* (April 1943).
———. "Malfeliĉo de l'demokrata mondo." N.a. (April 10, 1945).
———. "Monologoj de junaj geesperantistoj." *Esperanto bungaku* (November 1935).
———. "Nuna stato de japana proleta literaturo." *La mondo* (March–April 1936).
———. "Pri la lasta eklipso de la suno." *Infanoj sur tutmondo* (February–March 1936).
———. "Virina stato en Japanio." *La mondo* (March–April 1935).

ORIGINAL COLLECTED WORKS BY HASEGAWA TERU

Luchuan Yingzi. *En Ĉinio batalanta.* Chongqing: Koresponda Esperanto-Lernejo, 1945.
Verda Majo. *Flust' el uragano.* Chongqing: Heroldo de Ĉinio, 1941.
Includes "Al la tutmonda Esperantistaro"; "Amo kaj malamo"; "Batalante ili iras antaŭen"; "Du pomoj perditaj"; "En la maja ĉefurbo"; "Japanio—lando sub barbara regado"; "Profilo de japanaj studentoj"; "Tempo de anstataŭaĵoj"; "Venas la vintro, ne foras do l'printempo"; "Venko de Ĉinio estas ŝlosilo al la morgaŭo de la tuta Azio."

OTHER SOURCES

Agora Ōsaka, ed. *Hasegawa teru o tadoru tabi. Agora* 280 (December 2002).
———. *Yami wo terasu senko: Hasegawa Teru to musume Akiko. Agora* 253 (October 10, 1999).
———. *Yami wo terasu senkō II: Hasegawa Teru o shanhai jūkei ni shinobu. Agora* 296 (July 29, 2004).
Bown-Struyk, Heather, and Normal Field, eds. Introduction to *For Dignity, Justice and Revolution: An Anthology of Japanese Proletarian Literature.* Chicago: University of Chicago Press, 2016.
Coble, Parks M. *China's War Reporters: The Legacy of Resistance against Japan.* Cambridge, MA: Harvard University Press, 2015.
DeBoer, Stephanie. *Coproducing Asia: Locating Japanese-Chinese Regional Film and Media.* Minneapolis: University of Minnesota Press, 2014.
Esselstrom, Erik. "The Life and Memory of Hasegawa Teru: Contextualizing Human Rights, Trans/Nationalism, and the Antiwar Movement in Modern Japan." *Radical History Review* 101 (Spring 2008): 145–159.
Gong Peikang. "Verda Majo en Ĉinio (I)." *El popola Ĉinio,* no. 3 (1979): 16–19.

———. "Verda Majo en Ĉinio (II)." *El popola Ĉinio*, no. 4 (1979): 22–37.

———. "Verda Majo en Ĉinio (III)." *El popola Ĉinio*, no. 5 (1979): 24–27.

Hasegawa Teru henshū iinkai, ed. *Hasegawa Teru: Nicchū sensōka de hannichi hōsō o shita nihonjosei*. Osaka: Seseragi shuppan, 2007.

Ives, Peter. *Language and Hegemony in Gramsci*. London: Pluto Press, 2004.

Janton, Pierre. *Esperanto: Language, Literature, and Community*. Translated by Humphry Tonkin, Jane Edwards, and Karen Johnson-Weiner. Albany: State University of New York Press, 1993.

Ĵelezo [Ye Laishi, pseud.], ed. *Verkoj de Verda Majo*. Beijing: Ĉina Esperanto-Eldonejo, 1982.

Kageki, Tatsuya. "An Anarchist Woman's Ideological Conversion: How Mochizuki Yuriko Became a Nationalist in Manchuria." In *Women in Asia under the Japanese Empire*, edited by Jiajia Yang and Tatsuya Kageki, pp. 134–148. New York: Routledge, 2023.

Konishi, Sho. *Anarchist Modernity: Cooperatism and Japanese-Russian Intellectual Relations in Modern Japan*. Cambridge, MA: Harvard University Press, 2013.

Lu Yuanming. *Chūgokugo de nokosareta Nihon bungaku: Nit-Chū sensō no naka de*. Translated by Nishida Masaru. Tokyo: Hosei daigaku shuppankyoku, 2001.

Michielsen, Edwin. "Assembling Solidarity: Proletarian Arts and Internationalism in East Asia." PhD diss., University of Toronto, 2021.

Mitsui, Hideko. "Longing for the Other: Traitors' Cosmopolitanism." *Social Anthropology* 18, no. 4 (2010): 410–416.

Miyamoto Masao, ed. *Hasegawa Teru sakuhinshū: Hansen esuperanchisuto*. Tokyo: Nihon tosho sentā, 1994.

Miyamoto Masao and Ōshima Yoshio. *Historio de La Kontraŭreĝima Esperanto-Movado/Hantaisei esuperanto undō-shi*. Tokyo: Sanseidō, 1987.

Müller-Saini, Gotelind. "Hasegawa Teru alias Verda Majo (1912–1947): Eine Japanische Esperantistin im Chinesischen anti-Japanischen Widerstand." In *Cheng—All in Sincerity: Festschrift in Honour of Monika Übelhör*, edited by Denise Gimpel and Melanie Hanz. Hamburg: Hamburger Sinologische Gesellschaft, 2001.

Nakamura Kōhei. "Heiwa no hato—Veruda Maayo: Hansen ni shōgai wo sasageta esuperanchisuto Hasegawa Teru." *Kanagawa daigaku jinbungaku kenkyū johō*, no. 37 (2004): 55–66.

Sasamoto-Collins, Hiromi. "Facilitating Fascism? The Japanese Peace Preservation Act and the Role of the Judiciary." In *Fascism and*

Criminal Law: History, Theory, Continuity, edited by Stephen Skinner, pp. 163–189. Oxford: Hart, 2015.

Sexton, John. *Red Friends: Internationalists in China's Struggle for Liberation.* London: Verso, 2023.

Shibata Iwao. "Hasegawa Teru kenkyū: Nittchū sensō Chūgoku ni okeru hansen katsudō no kiseki." *Chiba kōgyō daigaku kenkyū hōkoku jinbunhen* 35 (1998): 107–155.

Takasugi Ichirō. *Chūgoku no midori no hoshi.* Tokyo: Asahi shinbun shuppan, 1980.

Tone Kōichi [Yoshida Susugu, pseud.]. *Teru no shōgai.* Yōmon-sha, 1969.

Yamada Yukiko. "Kōhai Hasegawa Teru." In Miyamoto, *Hasegawa teru sakuhinshū,* p. 203.

Zhao Xinli. "Nitchūsensō-ki ni okeru Chūgokukyōsantō no tainichi puropaganda senjutsu senryaku: Nipponhei horyo taiō ni miru '2-bu-hō' no imi." PhD diss., Waseda University, 2010.

Index

1911 Revolution, 45, 117
Adam ("Lanti"), Eugène, 94n39
alienation, 38, 40, 68, 73, 82–83
Al nova etapo, 76
arrest: of leftists, 4; of students, 4–5, 45, 142, 162; of war criminals, 169, 173; *see also under* Hasegawa Teru, arrest of
annationalism, 8, 94, 94n39, 124n3
antifascist, antifascism, 6, 7, 158: and Esperanto, 6, 131; as a global struggle, 4, 8, 114, 121, 124–125, 128
An Chunggŭn, 11
An Useng, 10–11. *See also* Elpin
Aonami An, 17
April 16 Incident, 4
Araki Sadao, 163, 165

Bahá'í religion, 7
Ba Jin, 57, 57n30
Beijing, 41, 43, 51, 60, 78, 107, 113
Bungaku annai, 3, 39n7

Cantonese: culture, 88–89; language: 8, 74, 79, 88, 98; women, 89–90
CCP: *See* Chinese Communist Party

censorship, 7, 16, 116, 139, 158
Chen Yuan, 76, 77, 94, 96
Chiang Kai-shek, 9, 10, 39n8, 49n24, 50n26, 83
China: People's Republic of, 13–14, 41n11, 43n15; Republic of, 45, 45n18, 49, 72. *See also under* Japan, invasion of China; amicable relations with China
Chinese: anti-Chinese sentiment, 31, 32, 35, 51, 91, 117, 145–146; culture, 89, 115, 123; food, 36, 88; immigration, 89
Chinese Communist Party (CCP), 9, 14, 37, 39n8, 42n12, 50n26; relations with the KMT, 9, 10, 13, 99, 125–126
Chinese Esperanto League, 41n11
Chinese Proletarian Esperantist Union, 8
Ĉinio hurlas, 8, 40n9, 41n11, 47, 47n20, 117
Chongqing, 10, 11, 44, 83, 99, 100, 101, 103n1, 105, 106, 107, 109, 126, 130, 133, 148, 167
Chūō kōron, 167
Clausewitz, Carl von, 51

180 Index

comfort women, 123
concessions (of Shanghai): the
  French Concession, 7, 35, 38,
  49, 53, 55–58, 113; the British
  Concession, 42. *See also* Safety
  Zone, the
communication: importance of,
  7–8, 38, 46, 134–135. *See also*
  language barrier/problem(s)
Comintern, 45

Dai Li, 10
danmin, 90, 90n38
democracy, 134–135, 169–174
Deng Keqiang, 45, 45n18, 77,
  90–93, 96, 97, 98
Deng Naiyan, 45n18
discrimination: class-based, 34, 35,
  53, 55, 90, 107, 150;
  gender-based, 90, 142,
  149–156; race-based, 6, 31,
  32, 34, 35, 38, 90, 129, 131

El popola Ĉinio, 41n11
Elpin, 11: "The Dove of Peace,"
  24–25. *See also* An Useng
En Ĉinio batalanta: See *Inside
  Fighting China*
Eroshenko, Vasily, 7
Esperanta literaturo, 5
Esperantist: as an identity, 6, 13,
  18, 31, 32, 40, 43, 85, 115,
  116–119, 121, 124–125
Esperanto: and antifascism/
  anti-imperialism, 6, 8, 32, 43,
  116–119, 124–125, 134; and
  anti-Japanese propaganda,
  93–94, 125; congresses,
  42–45, 77; and cosmopolitanism, 8; and Eurocentrism,
  17–18; democratic character
  of, 131–132, 135; difficulty for
  Chinese and Japanese speakers, 47; invention of, 3, 131;

and internationalism/transna-
  tionalism, 3, 8, 18, 31–32,
  116–119, 118, 125, 131; in
  Japan, 3; and leftist activism in
  East Asia, 3, 8, 118; meaning
  of, 18; as a networking tool,
  7–8, 46, 48; as a neutral/
  common language, 3, 6, 8,
  128, 131, 134, 135; as a
  nongovernmental movement,
  17, 135; pro-Japanese
  propaganda, 13, 124, 134; and
  proximity to English, 75; as a
  secret language, 36, suppression of, 118; as a revolutionary
  language, 8, 18, 124–125
"Espero, la," 29n1, 43, 43n14,
  127; lyrics to, 29, 30
European: anti-European sentiment, 61, 139–141, 143

Fascism: in Europe, 3, 32, 120,
  121, 129; in the Japanese
  Empire, 3–4, 32, 114, 128,
  129, 139–143, 144–148,
  161–167, 168–174; and
  language, 133–135
February 26 Incident, 162
"Fight Back to Our Old Home,"
  44n16, 44n22: lyrics of, 44, 48
Fighting China, 7, 76, 83, 97, 98,
  99, 108, 125; relation to
  Fighting France, 22n24
Flust' el uragano. See *Whisper from
  a Storm, A*
freedom, 1, 7, 43, 51, 62, 63, 90,
  114, 115, 117, 126, 135, 166
Fujimoto Tadayoshi, 4
Fujisawa Chikao, 124, 141, 141n2

Grabowski, Antoni, 43n14
Gramsci, Antonio, 8
"Great Wall Ballad, the," 48n21:
  lyrics of, 48

green (color of Esperanto), 6, 8, 30, 30n2, 32, 40, 43, 127; green star, 30n2, 40, 44, 47, 124, 129, 135; Green House, 92, 93, 94. *See also* Majo, Verda
Guangdong, 45, 94, 96, 97
Guangdong Esperanto Association, 94
Guangzhou, 9, 43, 63, 72, 73, 76, 77, 78, 80, 81 82, 83, 84, 88, 89, 93, 101, 121–122; revolutionary character of, 89, 90
Guo Moruo, 9–10, 41n10, 82–83, 82n36

Hankou, 9, 10, 44, 62, 63, 72, 76, 77, 78, 81, 82, 84, 85, 93, 94, 99, 100, 101: as the center of the Chinese resistance, 9, 10, 63, 76, 83; as a symbol of antifascism, 10
Hasegawa Teru: anecdotes, 2, 4–5; arrest of, 4–5, 73–75, 96; and Esperanto, 3, 5; childhood and schooling, 1–3; children (Xing and Xiaolan), 12, 13, 14; death, 13; deportation from China, 9–10, 96–99, 108; literary influence, 16–17; media portrayals, 11, 14–15, 103; as a radio announcer, 10, 11, 24, 102; as a symbol of progressive causes, 15–16; as a writer and translator, 2–3, 12, 13, 16, 19–20, 20n20, 39, 47, 85, 94, 98–99
Hearn, Lafcadio, 144, 145
Heroldo de Ĉinio, 40n9
Higashikuni Naruhiko, 169, 169n2, 172
Hitler, Adolf, 32, 121, 133, 135, 139
Hirohito (Emperor of Japan), 169, 169n2

Hirotsu Kazuo, 167, 167n3
homaranismo ("humanitism"), 127, 127n1, 132
Hong Kong, 9, 10, 63, 65, 74, 77, 94, 96, 96n40, 97, 98, 108: Hasegawa's description of, 71–72; Hong Kong foot disease, 78
Huang Xing, 45, 45n18
Huang Yihuan, 45–46, 45n18, 91

Ikeda Nariaki, 145
Ikeda Yuki, 6, 71n33, 94
Infanoj sur tutmondo, 5
Informacio, 120, 120n1
Inside Fighting China, 12, 14, 16, 17, 18, 19, 22n24; plan for further installments, 98–100
intermarriage: as an act of solidarity, 6, 32; prohibition of, 9, 75, 82, 96–97. *See also* marriage
International Association of Guangdong, the, 93–94
International language. *See* Esperanto.
International Settlement/concession(s), 49, 72. *See* concessions
Inukai Tsuyoshi, 4
Ishikawa Tatsuzō, 12
Ishikawa Takuboku, 81, 81n35
Ito Hirobumi, 11

Japan: amicable relations with China, 14, 117, 171; cultural connection to China, 113–114, 117; invasion of China, 4, 9, 13, 39n8, 43n13, 83, 121, 134, 149, 160, 164, 166, 170, 171; surrender and occupation, 13, 168–174
Japanese: acts of anti-militarism/antifascism, 6, 114, 121, 128, 158–159, 171; anti-Japanese sentiment, 38, 56, 75;

suppression of Chinese culture, 123; suppression of Korean and Taiwanese culture, 133; wives of Chinese nationals, 36, 37, 38, 52–53, 58, 82–83, 97

Japanese Communist Party, 57n30, 172n3, 173

Japanese Esperanto Institute, 5

Japanese People's Anti-War Alliance, 10, 71n33

Japanese Union of Proletarian Esperantists, 5

Justeco, 94

Kakushin, 150

Kaji Wataru, 6, 10, 70–71, 71n33, 94

Kiken shisō ("dangerous thoughts"), 4

Kishi Yamaji, 39n7

Klara Rondo ("Klara Circle"), 5

KMT, *See* Kuomintang

Kobayashi Erika, 17

Konoe Fumimaro, 143

Korean, 11, 134; *See also* comfort women

Kuomintang, 9, 10, 39n8. *See also under* Chinese Communist Party, relations with the KMT

Kusuri Kei, 33n3

labor: conditions in China, 34–35, 46; conditions in Japan, 4, 114, 147, 149–160, 164–165; labor service (compulsory student labor), 164–165

language barrier/problem, 38, 40, 46, 61, 63, 65, 66, 68, 81, 95, 96, 98, 116, 134–135

Lanti: *See* Adam ("Lanti"), Eugène

Latinxua movement, 41, 41n10, 79

Lenin, Vladimir, 159

Literatura gvido, la: See Bungaku annai

Luchuan Yingzi, 10, 20. *See* Hasegawa Teru

Liu Ren, 6, 9, 10, 13, 18, 32, 33–34, 34n4, 35–39, 41, 52, 54, 58, 59, 63, 65, 68–69, 70, 73–75, 77–78, 80–81, 82–83, 85, 93, 96

Lugou Bridge Incident, 9, 16, 43, 43n13, 44–45, 47, 48n21, 134

Lu Xun, 11, 41n10, 52n28

Majo, Verda ("Green May"), 1, 6, 25n1, 108; *See* Hasegawa Teru

Manchukuo, 6, 82

Manchurian Incident, 4, 49, 49n24, 52, 53, 59, 133, 141

Mangada, Julio, 8, 120, 120n1, 127–130

May: as a part of Hasegawa Teru's penname, 6, 25; connotations of, 25, 106–109

"May Flowers," 109; lyrics of, 49, 106

March 15 Incident, 3–4

"March of the Volunteers," 43n15, 50n25, 51n27, 109; lyrics of, 43, 50–51

Marco Polo Bridge incident. *See* Lugou Bridge Incident.

marriage: antimarriage 90, 92. *See also* intermarriage

Maruyama Yoshiji, 39n7

Miyako Shinbun, 165

Miyamoto Masao, 14, 19, 22n35

Mizuno Hamako, 4

Mochizuki Yuriko, 7

Modern girls, 148. *See also* women

mondo, la, 5, 41, 41n11

Mongolian, 134

Murofuse Kōshin 39, 39n7, 117

Mushanokōji Saneatsu, 166

Nabeyama Sadachika, 173

Nagato Yasu, 4–5

Index   183

Nakagaki Kojirō, 45n18
National Salvation Newspaper,
    90
Nanjing, 44n17, 62, 83, 133
Nara, 2, 4
Nara Esperanto Association, 3
New Fourth Army, 42n11
New Order, 117, 163–164. *See also*
    fascism
New Year, 83–85
Nihon hyōron, 39
Nippona Proleta Artista Federacio.
    See Zen Nihon Musansha
    Geijutsu Renmei
Nishimura Masao, 33n3
Northern Campaign, the, 82, 84

"Ode to the West Wind," 130
Okano Susumu, 172, 172n3, 173,
    173n4. *See* Sanzō Nosaka
Opium Wars, 89
Ōyama Shunpō, 4

Patriotic Women's Association,
    141, 145
patriotism, 1, 11–12, 115, 117,
    164
police, 4–5, 10, 36, 51, 61, 62,
    73–75, 87, 90, 91, 118, 139,
    140, 142, 150, 162–163; Sikh
    and Vietnamese officers of the
    Shanghai Municipal Police, 34,
    57; Tokyo Metropolitan
    Police, 45, 151, 154
Popola fronto, 120, 120n1
Potsdam Declaration, the, 169,
    172, 173
prostitution, 140, 141, 150, 162
protest, 9, 49–51, 86, 108, 114

refugees, 12, 53, 54–55, 57, 62–63,
    66–67, 84, 86, 113
Renn, Ludwig, 121, 121n2
Revuo orienta, la, 5

Safety Zone, the, 48, 53, 55, 62.
    Also see concessions
San Francisco Congress, the,
    134–135
Sano Manabu, 173
Sanzō Nosaka: *See* Okano Susumu
Sennacieca Asocio Tutmonda
    (SAT), 8, 94n39, 124, 124n3
SEL. *See* Shanghai Esperanto
    League
Seven Gentlemen, the, 50, 50n26
Shanghai: Hasegawa's opinion of,
    34–35; Battle of Shanghai, 9,
    47, 51, 56–58, 113, 120; fall
    of, 37, 60; intellectuals, 78, 93.
    See also Safety Zone,
    concessions
Shanghai Esperanto League (SEL),
    8, 42, 46, 56
Shanghai Incident, 37, 37n6, 53
Shantou, 69–71
Shelley, Percy Bysshe, 130n2
Shimazaki Tōson, 29
Shōwa emperor, the: *See* Hirohito
"Song of the National Salvation
    Army," 85, 37: lyrics of, 85
Spain, 8, 114, 121, 123, 128
Spanish Civil War: 120n1, 121n2,
    global implications of, 128
staple fibre (S. F.), 145, 145n2
suno, la, 124
Sun Yat-sen, 45
Sun Yat-sen University, 9, 76, 78,
    79, 92
Štimec, Spomenka, 17
students, 65, 68, 69, 76, 78, 79–80,
    86, 92, 93, 107; as a symbol of
    youth, 79, 92, 166–167; in
    wartime Japan, 114, 142,
    161–167
Suzuki Kantarō, 169, 169n2, 170

Taiwan, 79, 133, 172
"Taigô," 43, 43n14, 127

184 Index

Takasugi Ichirō, 14, 16
Tamanoi, 162
Tempo, 124
Tokyo, 2, 5, 15, 35, 36, 37, 39, 40,
44, 45, 64, 77, 78, 82, 85,
104n2, 108, 114, 118, 124,
127, 141, 142, 144, 150, 151,
152, 157, 162n1, 164
Tōyama Mitsuru, 45, 45n19

United States of America (US), 13,
170
Universal language, 29n1, 32. *See*
Esperanto

War of Resistance, 37n6, 60, 76,
98–99, 106, 125–126; global
implications of, 115, 118, 126;
See also Fighting China
Wang Jingwei, 44, 44n17, 107n2;
supporters of, 107, 170n2
Whisper from a Storm, A, 12, 16
White Russians, 53, 134
women: and antiwar/antifascist
activity, 158–159; in the
Esperanto movement, 79, 93;
and labor, 4, 5–6, 149–60; in
wartime Japan, 5–6, 142–142,
149–160; and emancipatory
struggles, 7, 89–90, 157–160;
role within the Japanese family

system, 149, 155, 156; and
workplace reform 6, 155, 158
Women's League for National
Defense, 145

Xi'an Incident, 39, 39n8, 49, 51
Xiao Cong, 84
Xiao Hong, 10
Xinhua ribao, 41

Yamakawa Hitoshi, 57, 57n30,
117
Yang Hucheng, 39n8
Ye Laishi, 5, 8, 10, 14, 19, 40–42,
40n9, 63, 76, 84–85, 92, 94
Yuan Shikai, 107–108
Yuan Zhu, 36
Yue Jiaxuan, 42
yum cha, 88–89

Zamenhof, Klara, 5
Zamenhof, Ludwik Lejzer, 3, 29n1,
43n14, 56, 120, 127, 127n1,
129, 131; Zamenhof Day, 44,
125, 127, 129
Zen Nihon Musansha Geijutsu
Renmei, 3
Zetkin, Clara, 5
Zhang Qicheng, 41–42, 41n11
Zhang Xueliang, 39, 39n8

About the Author

HASEGAWA TERU (1912–1947) was a Japanese human rights activist and Esperantist who, under the nom de plume Verda Majo (Green May), wrote and published searing criticisms of Japan's invasion of China in 1937 and its aftermath. Her autobiographical fragment *Inside Fighting China* is a celebrated work of Esperanto literature.

About the Translator

ADAM KUPLOWSKY is a translator based in Toronto. He previously translated *The Narrow Cage and Other Modern Fairy Tales* (2023), a collection of radical tales and fables by the Ukrainian storyteller and Esperantist Vasily Eroshenko.